W9-AVX-523

COMPREHENSIVE RESEARCH
AND STUDY GUIDE

BLOOM'S
MAJOR
SHORT
STORY
WRITERS

D. H.
Lawrence

EDITED AND WITH AN
INTRODUCTION BY HAROLD BLOOM

CURRENTLY AVAILABLE

BLOOM'S MAJOR SHORT STORY WRITERS

Anton Chekhov

Joseph Conrad

Stephen Crane

William Faulkner

F. Scott Fitzgerald

Nathaniel Hawthorne

Ernest Hemingway

O. Henry

Shirley Jackson

Henry James

James Joyce

D. H. Lawrence

Jack London

Herman Melville

Flannery O'Connor

Edgar Allan Poe

Katherine Anne Porter

J. D. Salinger

John Steinbeck

Mark Twain

John Updike

Eudora Welty

BLOOM'S MAJOR WORLD POETS

Maya Angelou

Robert Browning

Geoffrey Chaucer

Samuel T. Coleridge

Dante

Emily Dickinson

John Donne

T. S. Eliot

Robert Frost

Homer

Langston Hughes

John Keats

John Milton

Sylvia Plath

Edgar Allan Poe

Poets of World War I

Shakespeare's Poems & Sonnets

Percy Shelley

Alfred, Lord Tennyson

Walt Whitman

William Wordsworth

William Butler Yeats

COMPREHENSIVE RESEARCH
AND STUDY GUIDE

BLOOM'S
MAJOR
SHORT
STORY
WRITERS

D. H.
Lawrence

EDITED AND WITH AN INTRODUCTION BY HAROLD BLOOM

© 2001 by Chelsea House Publishers, a subsidiary of
Haights Cross Communications.

Introduction © 2001 by Harold Bloom.

Printed and bound in the United States of America.

First Printing
1 3 5 7 9 8 6 4 2

Library of Congress Cataloging-in-Publication Data
applied for

ISBN 0-7910-5947-2

Chelsea House Publishers
1974 Sproul Road, Suite 400
Broomall, PA 19008-0914

The Chelsea House World Wide Web address is
http://www.chelseahouse.com

Contributing Editor: Aaron Tillman

Produced by: Robert Gerson Publisher's Services, Santa Barbara, CA

Contents

User's Guide

This volume is designed to present biographical, critical, and bibliographical information on the author's best-known or most important short stories. Following Harold Bloom's editor's note and introduction is a detailed biography of the author, discussing major life events and important literary accomplishments. A plot summary of each short story follows, tracing significant themes, patterns, and motifs in the work, and an annotated list of characters supplies brief information on the main characters in each story.

A selection of critical extracts, derived from previously published material from leading critics, analyzes aspects of each short story. The extracts consist of statements from the author, if available, early reviews of the work, and later evaluations up to the present. A bibliography of the author's writings (including a complete list of all books written, cowritten, edited, and translated), a list of additional books and articles on the author and the work, and an index of themes and ideas in the author's writings conclude the volume.

⁓

Harold Bloom is Sterling Professor of the Humanities at Yale University and Henry W. and Albert A. Berg Professor of English at the New York University Graduate School. He is the author of over 20 books, including *Shelley's Mythmaking* (1959), *The Visionary Company* (1961), *Blake's Apocalypse* (1963), *Yeats* (1970), *A Map of Misreading* (1975), *Kabbalah and Criticism* (1975), *Agon: Toward a Theory of Revisionism* (1982), *The American Religion* (1992), *The Western Canon* (1994), and *Omens of Millennium: The Gnosis of Angels, Dreams, and Resurrection* (1996). *The Anxiety of Influence* (1973) sets forth Professor Bloom's provocative theory of the literary relationships between the great writers and their predecessors. His most recent books include *Shakespeare: The Invention of the Human,* a 1998 National Book Award finalist, and *How to Read and Why,* which was published in 2000.

Professor Bloom earned his Ph.D. from Yale University in 1955 and has served on the Yale faculty since then. He is a 1985 MacArthur Foundation Award recipient, served as the Charles Eliot Norton Professor of Poetry at Harvard University in 1987–88, and has received honorary degrees from the universities of Rome and Bologna. In 1999, Professor Bloom received the prestigious American Academy of Arts and Letters Gold Medal for Criticism.

Currently, Harold Bloom is the editor of numerous Chelsea House volumes of literary criticism, including the series BLOOM'S NOTES, BLOOM'S MAJOR DRAMATISTS, BLOOM'S MAJOR NOVELISTS, MAJOR LITERARY CHARACTERS, MODERN CRITICAL VIEWS, MODERN CRITICAL INTERPRETATIONS, and WOMEN WRITERS OF ENGLISH AND THEIR WORKS.

Editor's Note

My introduction centers upon *The Fox,* Lawrence's subtle story of a love triangle involving a quasi-Lesbian attachment.

As there are twenty-three critical views given here on five major tales and novellas, I will indicate only the illuminations that most aid me. On "The Prussian Officer," a study of displaced homosexuality and sadism, Keith Cushman is particularly helpful on Lawrence's double vision in the story. My remarks on "The Fox" can be contrasted with those of Kingsley Widmer, and Albert J. Devlin.

F. R. Leavis, perhaps Lawrence's classical critic, is very effective upon "The Captain's Doll," while "The Rocking-Horse Winner" is studied as myth by all of the exegetes.

St. Mawr, one of Lawrence's masterpieces, receives distinguished analyses from Richard Poirier and Sir Frank Kermode. ❀

Introduction

HAROLD BLOOM

D. H. Lawrence is now mostly out of favor and is particularly resented (with reason) by literary feminists. But he wrote two great novels in *The Rainbow* and *Women in Love*, and he was second only to Thomas Hardy among English poets of the Twentieth Century (setting aside the Anglo-Irish Yeats and the self-exiled-to-America Geoffrey Hill). Lawrence was also a prose-prophet and travel writer, but his most extraordinary achievement was as a tale-teller, whether in short stories like "The Prussian Officer" or in novellas like *The Man Who Died* and *The Fox*.

"The Prussian Officer" remains profoundly disturbing, and is a masterpiece of style and narration. It has particular value as a foil to *The Fox*, since the homoerotic, largely implicit drama of "The Prussian Officer" becomes almost wholly explicit in *The Fox*, a superb short novel of conflict between a man and a woman who compete for another woman.

The two girls, Banford and March, both nearing thirty, have a ambiguous relationship, evidently just short of sexual. Henry, the young soldier—nearly a decade younger than March—is a total antithesis to Banford. He is what once would have been called natural man: dignified, graceful, a born hunter, intense, instinctive. The love between March and Henry is immediate, but her history, her situation, and something recalcitrant in her nature combine to insure that their marriage will never be complete, in his sense of a desired union of souls. Poor Banford—doomed to defeat and to a near-suicidal death—nevertheless will remain a shadow upon Henry and March. The art of *The Fox* is beautifully dispassionate: Lawrence takes no side in the contest between Banford and Henry. And yet the storyteller is not disinterested; Lawrence's stance is defined by the presence and dark fate of the fox, with whom March associates Henry. One could argue that the young man wins his wife by slaying the fox, thus displacing the imaginative hold that the creature has upon March.

Lawrence is too grand a storyteller to indulge in any obvious symbolism, and we should not translate the fox into any simplistic reduction. He is a kind of demon, in the view of the two women, since his depredations make the existence of their farm dangerously marginal. March cannot slay him, because: "She was spellbound— she knew he knew her. So he looked into her eyes, and her soul failed her. He knew her, he was not daunted." As the young soldier's forerunner, he exposes March's vulnerability to male force, her almost unconscious discontent at her situation with Banford.

March's dreams prophesy the death of Banford, and the assumption of the fox's role by Henry. Lawrence is life's partisan, but he does not devalue Banford, who is no less life than Henry is. The subtlest portrait Lawrence gives us here is that of March, rather than of Banford or Henry. March's deep force seems more passive than it is. She will not kill the fox, and she will not renounce Henry irrevocably, but something in her goes into the dream-coffin with Banford. ❀

Biography of
D. H. Lawrence

D. H. Lawrence's short stories (he wrote over sixty) are among the finest in the language. While his realistic stories still provide a model of craft for contemporary writers, his visionary stories are unique. They are so much a product of his individual sense of life that they created no school of imitators.

D. H. Lawrence was born on September 11, 1885, in Eastwood, Nothinghamshire, England, the fourth child of Arthur John Lawrence, a life-long coal miner, and Lydia Beardsall Lawrence, daughter of a pensioned-off engine fitter. Lydia was a rather refined woman and immensely ambitious for her sons.

After attending the Beauvale Board School from 1891 until 1898, Lawrence won, at age twelve, a scholarship for Nottingham High School, where he studied until July 1901. After his graduation, he worked as a clerk at Haywood's surgical appliances factory in Nottingham; during the time of his employment there in 1901, he suffered the first of several attacks of pneumonia.

The following year, he frequently visited the Chambers family at Underwood, and he began his affectionate friendship with Jessie Chambers. Meanwhile, he left his clerk position, and for almost three years (1902–5), he worked as a teacher at the British School in Eastwood.

He started writing his first novel, *Laetitia,* in 1905–6 (it was published as *The White Peacock* in 1911). His first published work was a story called "A Prelude." (He submitted the story under the name Jessie Chambers.) It appeared in the *Nottinghamshire Guardian* in 1907. During these years, he also attended Nottingham University, obtaining his teacher's certificate in 1908.

That same year, Lawrence began working as an elementary teacher at Davidson Road School in Croydon, but before long he had to resign because he fell seriously ill with another bout of pneumonia.

The following years were eventful ones in Lawrence's life. His literary friend, Ford Madox Hueffer, began to publish his poems and stories in the *English Review* and also printed Lawrence's first novel,

The White Peacock, a study, among other things, of hypergamy (the aspiration of marrying into a social class above one's own). In 1910 Lawrence's affair with Jessie Chambers ended, his mother died, and he became engaged to his old friend Louise Burrows. (The engagement would eventually be broken off in 1912). His second novel, *The Trespasser* (1912), was published by Ducworth and Co., on the recommendation of their reader Edward Garnett.

Lawrence's unsettled, wandering life began in May 1912 when he eloped with Frieda Weekly, the aristocratic German wife of a professor who had taught Lawrence at Nottingham University. Lawrence and Frieda spent some time in Italy, where he wrote the final version of *Sons and Lovers,* published in 1913. In the same year his first volume of poetry, *Love Poems and Others,* appeared, and his first book of short stories, *The Prussian Officer and Other Stories,* was published in 1914.

After Frieda's complicated divorce, Lawrence and Frieda married in July 1914. At about the same time, he started important friendships with Catherine Carswell, Ottoline Morrell, Cynthia Asquith, Bertrand Russell, and E. M. Forster.

The years of World War I were a trying time in Lawrence's life. His intended emigration to the United States had to be postponed, partly because of his health, partly because of difficulties over Frieda's passport. They went to live at Zanor, near St. Ives, in Cornwall, but after twenty-one months of residence, they were ordered to leave by military authorities who suspected the couple of spying. Lawrence toyed with the idea of beginning an idealistic colony and tried to persuade his friends to join him, but before his plans could come to anything, his novel *The Rainbow* (1915) was published. The Public Morality Council immediately prosecuted Lawrence on obscenity charges, and demanded that an entire edition of the book be destroyed.

This book also caused a split between Garnett and Lawrence. Undeterred, in the following year, 1916, Lawrence finished its sequel, *Women in Love* (considered by novelist-critic Anthony Burgess to be one of the ten greatest novels of the century). This novel was rejected by publisher after publisher; it would not be published until after the First World War. (In the 1970s, Ken Russell made a movie of the book, setting the film in the 1920s.)

With the war over, Lawrence was still attracted to the idea of leaving Europe. In order to raise money from an American publisher, he began to write his splendid, if idiosyncratic, *Studies in Classic American Literature* (1923). The book clearly expresses Lawrence's realization that his future audience would be in America.

Meanwhile, Frieda went to Germany and then joined Lawrence in Florence; later on, they settled in Sicily. Private publication of *Women in Love* came out in 1920, and the following year Lawrence described his trip to Sardinia in his travel book *Sea and Sardinia* (1921). This book is the most charming and by far the best introduction to his oeuvre.

At last Lawrence's financial situations improved. His work began to sell in the United States, and a London publisher (Martin Secker) offered to reprint *The Rainbow* and to publish *Women in Love* (1921).

During the summer of 1920, which the Lawrences spent in Germany with Frieda's mother, Lawrence wrote *Fantasia of the Unconscious* (1922), a treatise on his psychological theories (which differ from Freud's); he also wrote the story "The Captain's Doll" during the same summer, and shortly afterward, he finished *Aaron's Rod,* a book he had begun in London in 1918; it was published in 1922. The next year one of the major achievements of his postwar exile appeared: a series of poems, *Birds, Beasts and Flowers.*

A period of travel followed this burst of creativity. The Lawrences accepted an invitation to visit the Brewsters, who were living in Ceylon, but very soon Lawrence became repelled by Ceylon. He and his wife went on to Australia, and then, weary of Australia as well, they accepted an invitation from Mabel Dodge. She had admired *Sea and Sardinia,* and now they joined her in Taos, New Mexico. However, Lawrence stayed only long enough to write, in six weeks, the strangest novel of his career—*Kangaroo.* He and his wife then traveled to California via the South Sea Islands. Finally, however, they settled in Taos in March 1923. But they spent the following summer at Chapala in Mexico, and there Lawrence began *Quetzalcoatl* (the first version of *The Plumed Serpent,* which would be published a few years later in 1926).

Frieda returned to London in July, and Lawrence followed her in November 1923. He continued to fantasize about forming an ideal community, and Catherine Carswell describes in *The Savage Pilgrimage* the famous Café Royal dinner, at which Lawrence invited his friends to return with him to Mexico to form the new society of which he had been dreaming since the war years. Only one of his friends followed him back to Mexico, however: Dorothy Brett, whose presence brought even more tension to the already complicated relationship between Mabel Dodge and Frieda.

Lawrence suffered his first bronchial hemorrhage in the winter of 1924–25; his health never improved. He moved to Kiowa Ranch (which Mabel Dodge Luhan gave to Frieda in exchange for his *Sons and Lovers* manuscript), and he subsequently used it as the setting for his short novel *St. Mawr.* In February 1925, he recovered enough to go to Oaxaca, Mexico, but while he was there he almost died of typhoid and pneumonia; in March he was diagnosed with tuberculosis.

The Lawrences returned to Europe in September 1925; *St. Mawr* was published at the same time. After a month in England, they moved to Spotorno near Genoa and afterward settled in Villa Mirenda, near Florence, in May of 1926. During this time, Lawrence started a friendship with Aldous and Maria Huxley, and here he wrote his meditation on the Etruscans, *Sketches of Etruscan Places.* This work is crucial to a deep understanding of his complete opus. Together with *The Man Who Died* and *Apocalypse,* it was posthumously published. In this work he looked to primitive societies to discover more elemental modes of living, using his findings to continue his attack on modern civilization.

Lawrence spent his last years writing and rewriting *Lady Chatterley's Lover,* his last novel, published privately in a limited edition in Florence in 1928, and in Paris in 1929. It appeared in England in 1932 as an expurgated version. (The complete text would not be published until 1959 in New York and 1960 in London.)

In 1929 police seized his unexpurgated typescript of *Pansies,* and Lawrence's health worsened as he continued his work on *Lady Chatterley's Lover.* Despite these difficulties, he completed the poignant story *The Escaped Cock* (later renamed *The Man Who Died*).

He and Frieda continued to go from place to place (Switzerland, the island of Port Cros, Bandol in the south of France, Paris,

Majorca, Bavaria) from June 1928 until Lawrence's death of tuberculosis at a sanatorium in Venice in 1930. Lawrence's last work, a commentary on the Book of Revelations, *Apocalypse,* was published posthumously.

"My great religion is a belief in the blood, the flesh, as being wiser than intellect. We can go wrong in our minds. But what our blood feels and believes and says, is always true," Lawrence wrote in his famous letter to Earnest Collings on January 17, 1913. As Anthony Burgess puts it in his biography of Lawrence, *Flame into Being:* "The center of Lawrence's response to the external world was the solar plexus, not the cerebral cortex." ❀

Plot Summary of
"The Prussian Officer"

Lawrence's first collection of stories, *The Prussian Officer and Other Stories*, was written between autumn 1907 and June 1913. All twelve stories in the collection were extensively revised or rewritten for book publication in June, July, and August of 1914.

"The Prussian Officer" is one of Lawrence's most famous short stories and has received considerable attention from literary critics who interpret it in various ways. Lawrence preferred his original title "Honour and Arms," as it was published in its two periodical appearances, and he was deeply annoyed when Edward Garnett, his early literary adviser, retitled it without his permission at the proof stage of the book.

The story opens with an unsurpassed description of a military march of some thirty kilometres. The Captain, "Herr Hauptman," is introduced as being 40 years old, with reddish hair that is graying slightly, and with a mustache over "a full brutal mouth"; his blue eyes flash with cold fire. The Captain is a Prussian aristocrat, the son of a Polish countess. Still, we are told, his outwardly assured looks may be deceiving, since he is in a state of constant inner tension that is only seen in the deep lines in his face, "which gave him the look of a man who fights with life."

The Captain's relationship with his orderly, Schöner, is simple at the beginning: just, distant, indifferent. But it will change. Even in his early stories, Lawrence establishes relationships whose rationale is irrational. The orderly is depicted as a youth of about 22, with dark expressionless eyes "that seemed never to have thought, only to received life direct through his senses, and acted straight from instinct." That unthinking quality seems to both enrapture and irritate his senior officer. The narrator adds the crucial sentence: "He did not choose to be touched into life by his servant." The reader must decide where the stress belongs: on "touched into life" or on "by his servant."

The officer watches and judges the youth's every movement. The mere opening of a bottle of wine or touching a loaf of bread can send a flash of hate through the officer's blood. Here, Lawrence reveals the officer's character as much as the youth's: the youth was not clumsy, but his instinctive sure movement, the grace of an unhampered young animal, irritates the officer. The slightest, most trivial thing—like the spilling of a bottle of wine—triggers strong emotional interchanges: the narrator tells us that the officer's eyes, "bluey like fire," held those of the confused youth for a moment. Afterward, "some natural completeness was gone, a little uneasiness took its place."

The two men become entangled in a psychological drama known only to them. The officer is strangely obsessed by the orderly, whereas the youth tries to distance himself, "to be left alone in his neutrality as servant." The youth's efforts are in vain; the officer learns the orderly has a girlfriend, and he goes mad with anger. He purposely keeps the orderly on duty in the evenings, finding deep satisfaction in interfering with his social life. But the officer's nerves are suffering. On one occasion he slings a belt in his servant's face.

The climax of the story comes when the orderly refuses to answer the officer when he asks him what he is doing with a pencil in his ear. This seems an irrelevant pretext for the Prussian to kick the youth from behind. When the officer repeats his question, threatening another kick, the youth says he has been writing poetry for his girl.

Lawrence's presentation of the inward struggle, the latent stirring of one's innate self, reaches its peaks in his description of the two characters' responses to this incident:

> The officer, left alone, held himself rigid, to prevent himself from thinking. His instinct warned him that he must not think. Deep inside him was the intense gratification of his passion, still working powerfully. Then there was a counteraction, a horrible breaking down of something inside him, a whole agony of reaction. He stood there for an hour motionless, a chaos of sensations, but rigid with a will to keep blank his consciousness, to prevent his mind grasping . . . He refused the event of the past night—denied it had ever been—and was successful in his denial. He had not done any such thing—not he himself. Whatever there might be lay at the door of a stupid, insubordinate servant.

Meanwhile,

> the orderly had gone about in a stupor all the evening. He drank some beer because he was parched, but not much, the alcohol made his feeling come back, and he could not bear it. He was dulled, as if nine-tenths of the ordinary man in him were inert. He crawled about disfigured. Still, when he thought of the threats of more kicking, in

the room afterwards, his heart went hot and faint, and he panted, remembering the one that had come. He had been forced to say 'For my girl.' He was much too done even to want to cry. His mouth hung slightly open, like an idiot's. He felt vacant, and wasted.

The next day maneuvers involve a long march in the hot sun, and the youth suffers from his bruises. He has one single intention now: to save himself. The Captain seems firmer and prouder with life. When the order to halt is placed, the officer orders the youth to bring him some food from the nearest inn. Lawrence gives a degrading description of the youth's obedience:

> . . . he turned in mechanical obedience, and set off at a heavy run downhill, looking almost like a bear, his trousers bagging over his military boots. And the officer watched this blind, plunging run all the way.

In the next paragraph the omniscient narrator juxtaposes the orderly's reaction:

> But it was only the outside of the orderly's body that was obeying so humbly and mechanically. Inside had gradually accumulated a core into which all the energy of that young life was compact and concentrated. He executed his commission, and plodded quickly back uphill. There was a pain in his head, as he walked, that made him twist his features unknowingly. But hard there in the center of his chest was himself, himself, firm, and not to be plucked to pieces.

The orderly attacks the officer, who is sitting on a tree-root. In almost erotic rapture, the two men fight, and the orderly chokes the Captain to death. Afterward, he pushes the body under the felled tree-trunks, takes the officer's horse, and rides out through the sun-blazed valley until he reaches the darkness of the woods. The author closes with these words: "Here his own life also ended."

The orderly dies in delirium, regaining only at moments clarity of consciousness. As his consciousness lapses, he has broken emotionally with the natural and human continuum. The last three paragraphs of this chapter are a wonderful description of the mind struggling to gain ground.

In the fourth, shortest section of the story, the bodies of the two men lie together, side by side. While one lies rigidly at rest, the other looks "as if every moment it must rise into life again, so young and unused, from a slumber." ❀

List of Characters in
"The Prussian Officer"

Hauptman, the Captain, is a Prussian aristocrat, the son of a Polish Countess. He seems haughty and overbearing, but the deep lines on his face show the irritable tension of his inner life. Occasionally he indulges himself with a mistress or prostitute, finding no pleasure in either. Almost unconsciously, he becomes aware of his young servant's vigorous presence and begins to give him sharp orders, taunts him with contempt, and bullies him. This moves the young man to kill him in a brutally intimate way.

Schöner, the orderly, is a youth of about 22 with strong, heavy limbs. His warm physical presence involuntarily imposes itself upon his master, the Captain, who is moved to flashes of irritation. Under the Captain's taunting and bullying, the youth tries to serve the abstract authority and avoid the man—but despite his effort, his hate grows. He murders the officer, but there his life also ends. He wanders away and dies from heat and hunger and thirst. ❀

Critical Views on
"The Prussian Officer"

KINGSLEY WIDMER ON THE ART OF NIHILISM

[Kinsley Widmer is the author of *Defiant Desire: Some Dialectical Legacies of D. H. Lawrence* (1992), and *Edges of Extremity: Some Problems of Literary Modernism* (1980). In this extract he discusses the destructive force of extreme experience.]

There is something more than homosexuality here. The sexual-sadism of the officer-servant relation rests on the covert sexual basis of all authority, but the point of narration is to follow the subjective change in the youth as his innocence loses contact with home, fellows, sweetheart, obedience and certainty. Forced to the extremity of feeling, the youth's rebellion is the gratuity of murder. The "passion of relief" with which he chokes the Captain to death, and then his solicitude for the destroyed body, has strong sexual elements; but his revenge is subordinate to the loss of purpose and the inversion of reality. The image of authority is dead, but one-fourth of the literal narrative remains to explore the subjective abyss of simple innocence as well as the unresolvable fatality that always marks the confrontation of innocence and authority.

A sensitive reading must account for the style and metaphoric order of the work as well as for the psychology and archetypal pattern of action and character. Take the opening paragraph of the story with its characteristic Laurentian intensification of physical sensation:

> . . . the valley, wide and shallow, glittered with heat; dark green patches of rye, pale young corn, fallow and meadow and black pine woods spread in a dull, hot diagram under a glistening sky. But right in front the mountains ranged across, pale blue and very still, snow gleaming gently out of the deep atmosphere. And towards the mountains, on and on, the regiment marched between the rye fields and the meadows . . . the mountains grew gradually nearer and more distinct. While the feet of the soldiers grew hotter, sweat ran through their hair under their helmets, and their knapsacks could burn no more in contact with their shoulders, but seemed instead to give off a cold, prickly sensation.

> He [the orderly] walked on and on in silence, staring at the
> mountains ahead, that rose sheer out of the land, and stood fold
> beneath fold, half earth, half heaven, the heaven, the barrier with slits
> of snow, in the pale bluish peaks.

This is not simply Lawrence's vivid sense of place and sensation. The repeated "on and on" towards the cool mountains—"the heaven" in the youth's mind—is the metaphoric direction of the story. The longing to escape the burden of hatred is what leads the youth to commit the murder, and it is part of the longing of this innocent to get away from passion and pain and the "dull hot diagram" of life.

Before returning to the later part of the story, we might recall the significance of the icy mountain image in Lawrence's work. Lawrence regularly uses the icy mountain, probably inherited as a romantic image of defiance, as a trope for the point beyond immediate life, the image of cosmic finality, the scene of life-denial. It so appears in passages in his travel writings. The snowy Alps provides the center of annihilation which separates the true lovers, who flee to the warm valley of the south, from the false lovers, who fatally identify themselves with the mountain scene, in *Women in Love*. An icy mountain is the scene of longing, and longed for death, of the self-destructive woman of "white-consciousness" whose sacrificial end concludes the novella "The Woman Who Rode Away." The demonic fascination of the remote and threatening mountains occurs in many other fictions: in the novella "St. Mawr" they appeal to the heroine who vehemently withdraws from modern life into the primitive harshness; in the story "The Princess" the rape of the heroine, and the death-love of the hero, takes place in the cold Rocky Mountains whose "wonder" has fascinated them. The chilling Abruzzi Mountains limit the love of the heroine of *The Lost Girl*. A snowy Mexico mountain attracts the hero of "The Flying Fish," a story fragment which is Lawrence's autobiographical piece on his near approach to death. And the crucial decision of initiation into fuller life of the hero in the novella "The Captain's Doll" is his lengthy and defiant rejection of the mountains and glaciers and everything they stand for, and his return to the warm valley, human purpose, and love. The longing of the youth in "The Prussian Officer" for the cool mountain heaven while yet in the hot plain of life leads to the destructive act and to annihilation.

At almost all points Lawrence's style insists that we be aware of the relation of person and natural scene, and it is his aesthetic as well as his metaphysical principle that everything in life must be "one living *continuum* with all the universe." After the young soldier has been carried away from normal life into the extreme of love and hate, only the image of authority has any relation to him. When he kills that he loses his last relation to the living universe. He no longer has a desire "to save himself"; and "nothing . . . could give him back his living place in the hot, bright morning." Thus all reality is lost: he is "disemboweled, made empty, a shadow creeping under the sunshine." He was only his passion; with that dead he is in a "blackish dream." The very ripeness of the summer scene, maintained from the opening paragraph of the story, turns to dissolution: "The air was too scented, it gave no breath. All the lush green-stuff seemed to be issuing its sap, till the air was deathly, sickly with smell of greenness." The human order dissolves with the natural order. His complete aloneness is his greatest pain: "He would not have minded anything, but he could not get away from the sense of being divided from the others." Later in his wanderings, thirsty and in need of help, he sees a peasant woman, but "he had no language with which to speak to her. She was the bright solid unreality."

—Kingsley Widmer, "D. H. Lawrence and the Art of Nihilism," *The Kenyon Review* 20, no. 4 (Autumn 1958): pp. 606–8.

GARY ADELMAN ON THE LIFE OF DENIAL

[Gary Adelman is the author of *Heart of Darkness: Search for the Unconscious* (1987), *Anna Karenina: The Bitterness of Ecstasy* (1990), *Snow of Fire: Symbolic Meaning in* The Rainbow *and* Women in Love (1991), and Jude the Obscure: *A Paradise of Despair* (1992). This extract is taken from his essay "Beyond the Pleasure Principle: An Analysis of D. H. Lawrence's 'Prussian Officer,'" published in 1963. Here he argues that "The Prussian Officer" is a dramatization of the aftereffects of 25 centuries of evasion and denial of life.]

As the prototype German officer, the Captain represents (in Lawrence's poetic vision) an exaggerated picture of modern man. He is a consequence, along with our mechanistic society, of 2,500 years of mechanical insistence on an ideal of impersonal service: "cold," "hostile," "cruel," "brutal"; "stiff," "tense," "rigid," "fixed"; never did he receive life "direct through his senses," never did he act "straight from instinct." He is one of the "unliving." The abrupt awakening of the man to desires he has with tragic insistence repressed and the consequence of these emotions which he can neither admit nor control are motivation for this masterpiece of Lawrence's short stories.

"Then the change gradually came." The Captain is suddenly aware of his young orderly's "vigorous, unconscious presence." He is aroused; "penetrated through [his] stiffened discipline"; "touched into life by his servant"; incapable, "in spite of himself," of regaining "his neutrality of feeling." His passion is intolerable, inadmissible. He is an officer, "a Prussian aristocrat, haughty and overbearing." His position dictates that he be impersonal; that he be "cold and just and indifferent" to an inconsequential servant. Schöner, the orderly, who has served him for more than a year, knew his duty, which "he took for granted, as he took the sun and the rain." He serves "the officer as if the latter were an abstract authority and not a man." Agitated and irritable, the Captain struggles to "keep himself hard to the idea of the service," but the "affair" gets out of hand. "He could not get away from the sense of the youth's person." "He could not rest when the soldier was away, and when he was present he glared at him with tormented eyes."

As the Captain's passion grows "madly irritable," Schöner grows "more mute and expressionless." The young soldier refuses "to be forced into a personal interchange with his master." The Captain is enraged. He begins to bully him, "using contempt and satire," and to take up as much of his time as possible. He seems to be going "irritably insane" in an obsessive desire to destroy the young soldier's instinctive, unhampered nature. "He was infuriated by the free movement of the handsome limbs, which no military discipline could make stiff." Schöner, whose every instinct "was to avoid personal contact," in spite of himself, feels his hatred grow in response "to the officer's passion."

The Captain spurs his servant's hatred, exulting in an intimacy of fear and bewilderment, at the same time succumbing to an uncontrollable desire to touch him: a glove in the face, then the end of a belt, then repeated kickings, always in the thighs and loins, and always at these times, "deep inside him was the intense gratification of his passion . . . working powerfully." Horribly brutalized, Schöner puts everything out of existence but the Captain. The Captain becomes "inevitable." He feels that he "must move under the presence of [his] figure." He feels that there are only "two people in the world . . . himself and the Captain." Finally, in an anguish of uncontrollable emotions, Schöner kills him.

Lawrence creates an orderly who is, before the "affair," childlike in his innocence. He lives instinctively, whereas the rigidly disciplined older man has repressed his nature, succumbing to a sterile way of life in which a mechanical obedience to the "idea of the service" destroyed all that was free in him. As an officer, the Captain is a master among men. Not only does he control and domesticate them, but also he denies his own nature and enslaves it completely. Athletic, graceful, Greek: he is apparently a man.

The Captain's life has been one long denial. He reveals his mortal want not only in his passion for Schöner, but also in the pleasure he takes in his command, the gratification he finds in "the hot smell of men," and in his love for horses. With his "long, fine hands and cultivated movements," his "white and slender" body, he "never married"—"no woman ever moved him to it" and he never moved a woman to it—he is obviously effeminate, finding his identity in an arbitrary, unnatural convention. His passionate hatred and love for Schöner are a consequence of a terrifying self-realization: that he is only the simulacrum of a man.

Schöner awakens in him a conflict of desires. The officer wishes to be loved—mastered—by the pristine, wild and unhampered, male vitality of his servant. But the mechanisms of his life continue despite him. He must command the men. And yet Schöner is not any man. With terrible destructive impact on the mental cosmos in which the officer has lived, as in an impenetrable shell, he has become an unconscious necessity. Driven by compassions he cannot deny, the Captain loses his equipoise. In agony he lusts after personal contact with Schöner. He manages somehow to keep his life organized, while gradually, torn apart by the struggle of unconscious demands with his militant will, he sinks (as Lawrence dramatizes it) into a perverse compromise. He brutalizes his servant with love, beats him for the gratification of the contact while at the same time remaining obedient to the ideal of his position. But even in this compromise there is design, as if his mind were forced to answer the needs of his unconscious. The Captain is intent on driving Schöner to a passion which must conclude with the orderly's killing him. This is to be the officer's fulfillment.

—Gary Adelman, "Beyond the Pleasure Principle: An Analysis of D. H. Lawrence's 'The Prussian Officer,'" *Studies in Short Fiction* 1, no. 1 (Fall 1963): pp. 9–11.

John B. Humma on Melville's *Billy Budd* and Lawrence's "The Prussian Officer"

[John B. Humma is the author of *Metaphor and Meaning in D. H. Lawrence's Later Novels*, published in 1990. In this extract, taken from his essay on Melville and Lawrence, he stresses the intriguing resemblances between *Billy Budd* and "The Prussian Officer."]

Since chronology is of no particular concern here, I will address myself first to "The Prussian Officer." Most of the details which I am about to recount have their approximate parallels in *Billy Budd*. The aristocratic Prussian captain is a tall, "handsome" man with an "irritable tension of his brow, which gave him the look of a man who fights with life." He is one of the first of Lawrence's "mind-conscious" types. The orderly, in direct contrast, is a young man who "seemed never to have thought, only to have received life direct through the senses, and acted straight from impulse." He moves, correspondingly, with "the blind, instinctive sureness . . . of an unhampered young animal." This "vigorous, unconscious presence" soon irritates the captain, and from the time the orderly accidently overturns a bottle of the captain's wine an "undiscovered feeling" holds between the two.

The orderly's "warm, full nature," the "free movement of his handsome limbs, which no military discipline could make stiff," increasingly annoys the captain, who "always kept himself suppressed." He cannot maintain any sort of neutrality toward the orderly, and finally must take action. The horrible beating he inflicts upon the orderly results from his jealous discovery that his subordinate has a girl friend. On maneuvers the following day, the captain can feel at ease for the moment, pleased and proud with his command, especially since "his orderly was among them in common subjection." The orderly's striking of the captain, after the captain has ordered him to fetch some refreshment, comes unpremeditated. Upon observing the captain's jaws working as he drinks, "the instinct which had been jerking at the young man's wrists suddenly jerked free. He jumped, feeling as if it were rent in two by a strong flame." As the captain lies dying (the orderly has broken his back), blood flows from his nostrils. The body, meanwhile, "twitched and sprawled there, inert. It was a pity *it* was broken. It represented more than the thing which had kicked and bullied him."

I have of course omitted a good deal. I have hardly touched, for instance, upon the Freudian aspects of the story, since they are at best tangential to the comparison. Similarly, in discussing *Billy Budd*, I will do little more than adumbrate the philosophical and moral problems represented by Billy and Claggart, the master-at-arms, but rather concentrate upon psychological issues.

Billy, as Melville describes him, personifies the "Handsome Sailor," a type which exhibits an "offhand unaffectedness of natural regality." He is one whose "moral nature was seldom out of keeping with the physical make." In these things, of course, he is not unlike the orderly. More significantly, however, he is "one to whom not yet has been proffered the questionable apple of knowledge," a statement pertinent both to the moral and to the psychological levels of the story. He has, in addition, little or no self-consciousness, or, as Melville puts it, "about as much as we may reasonably impute to a dog of St. Bernard's breed." He is "a sort of upright barbarian, much such perhaps as Adam presumably might have been ere the urbane serpent wriggled into his company."

The serpent in this instance is John Claggart, the master-at-arms. Like the Prussian officer, Claggart is tall and "no ill-figure on the whole." His outstanding physical feature, excepting his heavy protruding chin, is his brow, a characteristic, as Melville says, with usual understatement, of "more than average intellect." Lawrence, we recall, had remarked upon *his* officer's brow, stating that it was the brow of a man who "fights with life," a man such as Claggart is. Like the captain, moreover, the master-at-arms is rumored to have been of aristocratic background, to have been, in fact, a *chevalier*. A clue to his character is his complexion: the pallor "seemed to hint of something defective or abnormal in the constitution and blood."

As in "The Prussian Officer," a confirming incident crystallizes the antagonism. In Lawrence's story the incident is the spilled bottled of wine; in Melville's it is the spilled container of soup. The incident indicates to the reader the fact that Claggart is "secretly down on" Billy. The master-at-arms' subsequent "monomania" for getting even with his subordinate falls into the same pattern as the captain's monomania for persecuting the orderly. What riles Claggart most— and here the shades of "The Prussian Officer" loom large—is more than merely Billy's "significant personal beauty." Claggart's paranoid reaction almost precisely parallels the officer's:

> Nor, as directed toward Billy Budd, did it partake of that streak of apprehensive jealousy that marred Saul's visage perturbedly brooding on the comely young David. Claggart's envy struck deeper. If askance he eyed the good looks, cheery health, and frank enjoyment of young life in Billy Budd, it was because these went along with a nature that, as Claggart magnetically felt, had in its simplicity never willed malice, or experienced the reactionary bite of that serpent. . . . To be nothing more than innocent! Yet in an aesthetic way [Claggart] saw the charm of it, the courageous free-and-easy temper of it, and fain would have shared it, but he despaired of it.
>
> With no power to annul the elemental evil in himself, though readily enough he could hide it; apprehending the good, but powerless to be it; a nature like Claggart's surcharged with energy as such natures almost invariably are, what recourse is left to it but to recoil upon itself.

Melville's understanding here of the effects which sustained repression works upon the individual is every bit the equal of Lawrence's.

The presence also of the related qualities of prudence and secretiveness go hand-in-glove with Claggart's paranoia, as they do with the captain's:

> But in view of the greediness of hate for pabulum it hardly needed a purveyor to feed Claggart's passion. An uncommon prudence is habitual with the subtler depravity, for it has everything to hide. And in

case of an injury but suspected, its secretiveness voluntarily cuts it off from enlightenment or disillusion; and, not unreluctantly, action is taken upon surmise as upon certainty. And the retaliation is apt to be in monstrous disproportion to the supposed offense; for when in anybody was revenge in its exactions aught else but an inordinate usurer.

Both the master-at-arms and the captain suppress any outward display of their conflicts. The captain, in fact, in his duties, "knew himself to be always on the point of breaking out." Like Claggart, however, he always manages to contain himself.

The details surrounding Billy's striking of Claggart and Claggart's death itself also parallel the details of the captain's death in "The Prussian Officer." Like the orderly's attack upon the captain, Billy's blow is spontaneous, impulsive. Notably, it is delivered to the forehead, "so shapely and intellectual-looking a feature in the master-at-arms." Melville even uses the same word as Lawrence to describe the corpse's most evident condition: "inert." Finally, in "The Prussian Officer," Lawrence even describes the blood that issues from the officer's nose, just as Melville similarly describes the blood that flows from Claggart's mouth and ear.

To pull together, then, the correspondences, we find that both subalterns are unconscious types, natural and spontaneous in their actions and innocent of knowledge. Their officers, on the other hand, are acutely *conscious* individuals who repress their instincts. Both are characterized by intellects that have turned calculative, or mechanical. Both grow envious of the natural perfection represented in their subordinates, and since they are reminded by them of their own constitutional deficiencies, seek to destroy this naturalness by bringing the two younger men into their control. These attempts, of course, result in the destruction of the officers themselves, the details of which, as we have seen, are quite similar.

Melville's psychological implications in *Billy Budd* suggest Dostoyevsky, especially the Dostoyevsky of *Notes from Underground*, and Nietzsche—just two contemporaries who had their say about conscious *versus* unconscious behavior. And most significantly before them there had been Blake, whose prophecies abound in spectres tormented by the curse of self-consciousness. Nietzsche had written that "this growing consciousness" is a "disease," and declared that "we could in fact think, feel, will, and recollect, we could otherwise 'act' in every sense of the term, and nevertheless nothing of it would require to 'come into consciousness.'" According to Nietzsche, the *true* aristocratic man (unlike the master-at-arms and the captain, *false* aristocratic men) is sincere and lives in confidence and openness. His opposite, on the other hand, the resentful man, lacks all sincerity and openness: "His soul squints; his mind loves hidden crannies, tortuous paths and backdoors, everything secret appeals to him as *his* work, *his* safety, *his* balm; he is a past master in silence, in not forgetting, in waiting." Nietzsche has, in fact, portrayed Urizen as described in Blake's *The Book of Urizen*:

> Lo, a shadow of horror is risen
> In Eternity! Unknown, unprolific!
> Self-closed, all-repelling: What Demon
> Hath form'd this abominable void
> This soul-shudd'ring vacuum?—Some said
> "It is Urizen", But unknown, abstracted
> Brooding, secret, the dark power his.

Urizen is a prototype for Lawrence's captain and Melville's master-at-arms, modified only slightly to fit fresh circumstances. With his squinting, envious soul, he is Nietzsche's resentful man, the "past master in silence, in not forgetting, in waiting."

—John B. Humma, "Melville's *Billy Budd* and Lawrence's 'The Prussian Officer': Old Adams and New," *Essays in Literature* 1, no 1 (Spring 1974): pp. 83–86.

Keith Cushman on Lawrence's Dualistic Vision

[Keith Cushman edited three books on Lawrence: *Letters of D. H. Lawrence and Amy Lowell 1914–1925*, published in 1985, *Challenge of D. H. Lawrence* (1990), and *D. H. Lawrence's Literary Inheritors* (1991). He is also the author of *D. H. Lawrence at Work: The Emergence of the Prussian Officer Stories* (1978), from which this extract is taken. Here he examines Lawrence's artistic breakthrough with "The Prussian Officer."]

"The Prussian Officer" marks a significant breakthrough in Lawrence's art. Some critics, noticing the differences between the magazine and book versions of the tale, have talked about Lawrence's skill in revision as a way of accounting for the breakthrough. However, if they had examined a revised holograph of the story owned by Humanities Research Center of the University of Texas at Austin, they would have reached a strikingly different conclusion. Although sixty years have passed since Lawrence wrote this story, some of the most basic groundwork for critical appraisal still needs to be laid. In contrast, a study of the development of "The Thorn in the Flesh" offers a particularly radiant example of Lawrence's remarkable—and by this time familiar—growth at this crucial point of transition. ⟨. . .⟩

"The Prussian Officer," which is almost certainly the inspiration for Hemingway's little short story "A Simple Enquiry," has proven curiously elusive to critics. It has been discussed in terms of psychological theory, homosexuality and *Blutbrüderschaft*, and German militarism. A letter Lawrence wrote Garnett in the autumn of 1912 bears directly on the homosexual element of the story:

> I want to get into a corner and howl over the *Jeanne d'Arc* [a play written by Garnett]. Cruelty is a form of perverted sex. . . . And soldiers, being herded together, men without women, never being *satisfied* by a woman, as a man never is from a street affair, get their surplus sex and their frustration and dissatisfaction into the blood, and *love* cruelty. It is sex lust fermented makes atrocity.

In "The Prussian Officer," clearly enough, "sex lust fermented makes atrocity." The homosexual implications of the tale seem to be purposive, and a case can be made for interpreting the story in the light of psychological speculation and even of antimilitarism. However, I feel that Lawrence's sensibility is engaged at a deeper level.

"The Prussian Officer" is a fully achieved embodiment of Lawrentian metaphysic—of the dualistic vision so centrally significant to his best art. The Captain and his orderly are a complementary pair. The Captain, dominant and masculine, is fair, tall, and slender, with challenging blue eyes. Schöner, submissive and feminine, is short and swarthy, with heavy limbs and receptive dark eyes. These pairs of opposites function within the larger framework of antitheses that give the story structure: the valley and the mountains, heat and cold, life and death. The orderly has "dark, expressionless eyes, that seemed never to have thought, only to have received life direct through his senses, and acted straight from instinct." In the story, his awakening into consciousness is a violent experience that produces murder and his own death.

Lawrence's dualistic habit of mind has often been remarked, and critics are coming to realize its critical importance in his art and thought. The *Study of Thomas Hardy*, written in 1914 after the final revision of the *Prussian Officer* stories, is primarily an occasion for Lawrence to explore aspects of his dualistic universe. The final *Prussian Officer* revision is of course part of the same creative moment. The interesting point here is that the sexual and metaphysical polarities of "The Prussian Officer" itself predate both the first draft of *The Rainbow* and the *Study of Thomas Hardy*. In writing the story, he seems to "find" the metaphysic complete and fully articulated. The dualistic vision at the heart of the story is a version of the dynamic polarity between the Brangwen men and the Brangwen women. It also prefigures the dualistic speculations of such works of the twenties as *Fantasia of the Unconscious*.

Schöner, the young soldier of "The Prussian Officer," can also be found playing the role of a Bavarian peasant in "The Crucifix Across the Mountains," the first essay of *Twilight in Italy*. The earlier version of the piece, "Christs in the Tirol," was written in August or September of 1912 and was first published in the *Saturday Westminster Gazette* in March 1913, but the peasant emerged only when Lawrence transformed the piece into "The Crucifix Across the Mountains" for inclusion in the travel book. This revision probably dates from the autumn of 1915, over two years after the composition of the story. The language and symbolic structure of the story are taken over intact into the travel essay, and Lawrence's evocation of the Brangwen men also comes to mind. The peasant's body is a "hot welter of physical sensation," his mind is flushed "with a blood heat, a blood sleep." This "flow of sensuous experience" at last "drives him almost mad." In contrast, "overhead there is always the strange radiance of the mountains": "the ice and the upper radiance of snow are brilliant with timeless immunity from the flux and the warmth of life." "The Prussian Officer" is the story of the journey Schöner makes from the warm valley of life to the icy eternity of death when he is awakened from his "sleep, this heat of physical experience" by his captain. Schöner's progression to violence and death parallels the peasant's "crucifixion." As in so much of Lawrence's best work, the crucifixion is the tragic split between our mental and sensual being.

A reader does not need to know about Lawrence's dualistic vision or quasiphilosophical speculation in order to respond to "The Prussian Officer." Lawrence successfully translates his ideas into a compelling, almost expressionist, narrative charting the course of an intense relationship between two men. Theory is not obtrusive, but is does form the foundation of the story. "The Prussian Officer" is a splendid early example of the interplay of Lawrentian art and metaphysic. The metaphysic involved anticipates *The Rainbow* and Lawrence's greatest work as a novelist.

—Keith Cushman, *D. H. Lawrence at Work: The Emergence of the Prussian Officier Stories.* (Charlottesville: University Press of Virginia, 1978): pp. 168, 169–72.

Barry J. Scherr on Lawrentian Allegory

[Barry J. Scherr is the author of the book *D. H. Lawrence's Response to Plato: A Bloomian Interpretation* (1995). In this excerpt taken from his article published in *Recovering Literature* he argues that although "The Prussian Officer" has received considerable attention from literary critics, none of them has dealt with the story's profound allegorical range "that enhances its greatness as a work of art."]

Lawrence himself had a consummate understanding of allegory. In his own outstanding literary criticism, Lawrence provides us with a working definition of allegory:

> Allegory is narrative description using . . . images to express certain definite qualities. Each image means something, and is a term in the argument and nearly always for a moral or didactic purpose, for under the narrative of an allegory lies a didactic argument, usually moral.

What is the allegory in "The Prussian Officer"? To answer this question, it is necessary to determine what "definite qualities" are expressed in "The Prussian Officer" and what "images" are used to present these qualities. Finally, it will be possible to state precisely what the "didactic argument" of "The Prussian Officer" is; and our elucidation of this "didactic argument" can only serve to illuminate the meaning and greatness of this short story.

It is evident that the "definite qualities" dealt with in "The Prussian Officer" are personified by the Prussian officer, Herr Hauptmann, and his orderly Schoner. Furthermore, it is clear that, as a result of their respective qualities, there exists a significant connection between the two men—a connection rooted in animosity:

> The orderly felt he was connected with that figure moving so suddenly on horseback: he followed it like a shadow, mute and inevitable and damned by it.

Thus at this early stage of his story Lawrence tells us that there is a connection of hostility, of conflict, between the two men, and the orderly is at this point of the story clearly losing the battle to Herr Hauptmann, the Captain, whose power has "damned" the underdog orderly.

But what are the "qualities" that the underdog orderly personifies in this allegory? In his description of the orderly Lawrence tells us:

> He had strong, heavy limbs, was swarthy, with a soft, black, young moustache. There was something altogether warm and young about him. He had firmly marked eyebrows over dark, expressionless eyes, that seemed never to have thought, only to have received life direct through his senses, and acted straight from instinct.

Lawrence presents the orderly in terms of darkness (he is swarthy with dark eyes), sensuality (he "received life direct through his senses"), mindlessness (he has "dark, expressionless eyes, that seemed never to have thought"), and instinct (he "acted straight from instinct"). Indeed, the orderly is nothing less than an avatar of the "blood-consciousness" that Lawrence describes in his "blood-consciousness" letter to Bertrand Russell:

> there is another seat of consciousness than the brain and the nerve system: there is a blood-consciousness which exists in us independently of the ordinary mental consciousness, which depends on the eye as its source or connector. There is the blood-consciousness, with the sexual connection, holding the same relation as the eye, in seeing, holds to the mental consciousness. One lives, knows, and has one's being in the blood, without any reference to nerves and brain. This is one half of life, belonging to the darkness.

With his darkness and his powerful instinct, the orderly is surely the representative of the dark, sexual "blood-consciousness." As the orderly's adversary, the Captain is the embodiment of that mode of consciousness which is essentially antithetical to the vital "blood-consciousness"; Lawrence makes this clear in his description of the Captain: the "anti-life" Captain has "the look of a man who fights with life." For Lawrence at this stage in his thought, the "anti-life" way of consciousness is that of the "mental consciousness": because modern man has let the "mental consciousness" predominate, the life of Western civilization is imperiled. As Lawrence expresses it in his letter to Russell:

> And the tragedy of this our life, and of your life, is that the mental and nerve consciousness exerts a tyranny over the blood-consciousness, and that your will has gone completely over to the mental consciousness, and is engaged in the destruction of your blood-being or blood-consciousness, the final liberating of the one, which is only death in result.

As the anti-life force in the story, the Prussian officer has no enthusiasm for the sexual realm that is the essence of the "blood-consciousness":

> Now and then he took himself a mistress. But after such an event, he returned to duty with his brow still more tense, his eyes still more hostile and irritable.

Sex has no salubrious effect on the Prussian officer with his "mental" will, symbolized by the "cold fire" in his light-blue eyes. But the warm, dark-eyed orderly finds great solace in his sexual relationship with his sweetheart:

> The two walked together, rather silently. He went with her, not to talk, but . . . for the physical contact. This eased him, made it easier for him to ignore the Captain; for he could rest with her held fast against his chest. And she, in some unspoken fashion, was there for him. They loved each other.

Thus sexual love makes life bearable, even worthwhile, for Schoner; in true "blood-consciousness" fashion, his contact with his woman persists in its power over him, even when she is far away from him, in the manner adumbrated by Lawrence in his letter to Russell where Lawrence explains the enduring presence of the "blood-consciousness" between him and his woman:

> . . . when I take a woman, then the blood-percept is supreme, my
> blood-knowing is overwhelming. There is a transmission, I don't
> know of what, between her blood and mine, in the act of connection.
> So that afterwards, even if she goes away, the blood-consciousness
> persists between us.

The "blood-consciousness" and the male-female connection that transmit it are only provocative enemies to the "anti-life" Prussian officer, who soon becomes infuriated by the orderly's "young, vigorous, unconscious presence." With his sexuality and spontaneity, the orderly is recognized by the officer as his antithetical adversary. It takes time for the orderly to realize that the Captain is his mortal enemy, but finally Schoner understands that the supreme relationship in his life is the hate between him and the Captain: "It was between him and the Captain. There were only the two people in the world now—himself and the Captain." The Captain, having just brutally beaten Schoner in a fit of will and rage, has placed the orderly's very psychic being in jeopardy: "The orderly . . . felt himself put out of existence. He stood still for a moment submitting to his own nullification—then he gathered himself, seemed to regain himself, and then the Captain began to grow vague, unreal, and the younger soldier's heart beat up. He clung to this situation—that the Captain did not exist—so that he himself might live."

Thus the orderly comes to conclude that he is involved in a life-and-death struggle with the Captain. The orderly wants "to save himself"; he determines that the only way to do this is by killing the Captain. The Captain is the "dominant figure," while the orderly is now "a nonentity." Nonetheless, before long the orderly's instinctive "blood-consciousness" power revives him to such an extent that he actually gains the strength to kill the Captain. The orderly's slaying of the Captain is certainly presented as the victory of the "blood-consciousness" over the "mental consciousness." Killing the Captain with his bare hands, the orderly employs the strength of "blood-consciousness"; "He did not relax one hair's breadth, but, all the force of all his blood exulting in his thrust, he shoved back the head of the other man, till there was a little 'cluck' and a crunching sensation . . . Heavy convulsions shook the body of the officer, frightening and horrifying to the young soldier. Yet it pleased him, too. . . ." The orderly's "blood" in all its power rejoices in killing the Captain, the representative of the "mental consciousness." After the event the orderly is glad: "In his heart he was satisfied. He had hated the face of the Captain. It was extinguished now. There was a heavy relief in the orderly's soul. That was as it should be."

But the orderly's triumph is short-lived; as Lawrence cryptically remarks: "Here his life also ended." Indeed, the orderly dies only hours after his victory over the Captain. Minutes after he kills the Captain, the orderly senses that for him too it is the end of the world: "It surprised him that the leaves were glittering in the sun. . . . For him a change had come over the world. But for the rest it had not. . . . Only he had left it." In losing his feeling of contact with the everyday world, the orderly becomes more and more closely identified with the dark "blood-consciousness": ⟨. . .⟩

Thus the Lawrentian allegory in "The Prussian Officer" advocates perpetual creative conflict between the two forces of blood-consciousness and mental consciousness; in "The Prussian Officer," the *end* of the conflict brings disaster to both mental consciousness and blood-consciousness. But, as Lawrence concludes his story, he expresses the hope that the blood-consciousness and its representative the orderly will be resurrected sometime in the near future. Thus the dead body of the orderly looks "as if every moment it must rouse into life again, so young and unused, from a slumber." Lawrence's sympathies lie with the blood-consciousness symbolized by the orderly; but Lawrence knows that without the mental consciousness the blood-consciousness cannot endure—and Lawrence communicates his knowledge in the allegory of "The Prussian Officer," where Lawrentian thought about the "stable equilibrium by the opposition of the other" takes the form of great short fiction.

—Barry J. Scherr, "'The Prussian Officer': A Lawrentian Allegory," *Recovering Literature* 17 (1989): pp. 33–37, 40.

Plot Summary of
The Fox

Shortly before setting off on his journey to Ceylon, Australia, and America, in 1921, D. H. Lawrence revised a number of stories for a collected volume titled *England, My England*. At the same time he wrote three "novelettes," "The Captain's Doll," *The Fox*, and "The Ladybird." From his correspondence we can gather that he began *The Fox* in November 1918. The short version of *The Fox*, published first in *Hutchinson's Story Magazine* in 1920, was entirely transformed by an addition more than twice as long as the original story. In November 1921, Lawrence wrote in a letter, "I put a long tail on 'The Fox.'"

Lawrence opens the tale with a description of the farm. Two women, known throughout the story by their last names, Banford and March, run Bailey farm. Both are around 30 years old, but while Jill Banford is small, thin, and delicate, Ellen March is more robust, with the skills for carpentry and joinery; she is, in effect, "the man around the place."

The tale takes place during the war, and the reader soon learns that because of the war conditions, the women have trouble keeping the farm going. Adding to their troubles, a fox has been preying on the chickens at the farm, carrying off the hens under the very noses of Banford and March, who are becoming disheartened.

The turning point of the story comes one night when March, in her usual absentminded way, keeps guard with a gun under her arm. As she faces the fox, she shifts to another plane of reality.

> He was looking at her. His chin was pressed down, and her eyes are looking up. They met her eyes. And he knew her. She was spellbound. She knew he knew her. So he looked into her eyes, and her soul failed her.

Over the next few months, we are told, the fox dominates her unconscious mind. March is spellbound by his image.

One November evening, the time of the year both girls dread, a young soldier not more than 20, Henry Grenfel, shows up at the farm. He was born and bred in Cornwall, and five years ago he lived at the Bailey farm with his now deceased grandfather. Though at the beginning Banford is highly suspicious of him, she invites him to stay for dinner. Later, after a brief discussion between the women, he is allowed to lodge at the farm and help them. However, March instantly identifies him with the fox:

> But to March he was the fox. Whether it was the thrusting forward of the head, or the glisten of fine whitish hairs on the ruddy cheekbones, or the bright, keen eyes, that can never be said: but the boy was to her the fox, and she could not see him otherwise.

Meanwhile, Henry is irresistibly drawn to March. He feels:

> There was a secret bond, a secret thread between him and her, something very exclusive, which shut out everybody else and made him and her possess each other in secret.

Being young and inexperienced, he doesn't hesitate to ask her to marry him. At first she distrusts his motives, but later on she inwardly feels his influence on her. Banford and he, however, become antagonists; he begins to "dislike her with an acid dislike."

Lawrence now uses a new device to present the unconscious workings of the psyche—dreams. March dreams of Banford as dead.

After he shoots the fox, March admits to herself her desire for Henry and agrees to marry him sometime before Christmas when he comes back from military camp. Banford is infuriated. The narrator reveals March's inner thoughts:

> March looked at him wistfully. She wished she could stay with him. She wished she had married him already, and it was all over. For oh, she felt suddenly so safe with him. She felt so strangely safe and peaceful in his presence. If only she could sleep in his shelter, and not with Jill. She felt afraid of Jill. In her dim, tender state, it was agony to have to go with Jill and sleep with her. She wanted the boy to save her. She looked again at him.

And a page later the reader witnesses another of March's interior landscapes:

> . . . as the train drew away, she (March) was left feeling intensely forlorn. Failing his physical presence, she seemed to have nothing of him. And she had nothing of anything. Only his face was fixed in her mind: the full, ruddy, unchanging cheeks, and the straight snout nose, and the two eyes staring above. All she could remember was how he suddenly wrinkled his nose when he laughed, as a puppy when he is

playfully growling. But him, himself, and what he was—she knew nothing, she had nothing of him when he left her.

Nine days after his departure, Henry receives a letter from March, stating the impossibility of their marriage. Henry, with youthful urgency, requests leave and is granted one from his superior, Captain Berryman. He returns to the farm, because, "he wants the woman, he has fixed like doom upon having her."

He finds the women struggling to fell a tree. He offers to finish the job and warns Banford to move away before he fells the tree, but she refuses to move. Lawrence intends again to show the inner force of life at work.

> He looked at her again. She was wiping her hair from her brow again, with that perpetual gesture. In his heart he had decided her death. A terrible still force seemed in him, and a power that was just his. If he turned even a hair's breadth in the wrong direction, he would lose the power.
> "Mind yourself, Miss Banford," he said. And his heart held perfectly still, in the terrible pure will that she should not move.
> "Who me, mind myself?" she cried, her father's jeering tone in her voice. "Why, do you think you might hit me with the axe?"
> "No, it's just possible the tree might, though," he answered soberly. But the tone of his voice seemed to her to imply that he was only being falsely solicitous and trying to make her move because it was his will to move her.
> "Absolutely impossible," she said.
> He heard her. But he held himself icy still, lest he should lose his power.

The tree hits Banford and she falls dead. The boy knows, we are told, that the inner necessity of his life is fulfilling itself. March marries him and they plan to leave for Canada.

But by the time the "long tail" of the story ends, the ambiguous tension reaches its height. March feels she has failed. She cannot any more exert herself in love. "She has been all her life reaching, reaching, and what she reached for seemed so near, until she had stretched to her utmost limit. And then it was always beyond her. Always beyond her, vaguely, unrealisably, beyond her, and she was left with nothingness."

As for Henry, "he wanted her to commit herself to him, and to put her independent spirit to sleep. He wanted to take away from her all her effort, all that had seemed to her very raison d'être. He wanted to make her submit, yield, blindly pass away out of her strenuous consciousness."

How (and if) they solve the riddle of their emotional existence is left untold. ❀

List of Characters in
The Fox

Jill Banford is a small delicate woman of nearly 30 years old. With her friend Nellie March, she takes on a farm. Banford is the principal investor, since her father, a tradesman, gave her money to start her life. When the young soldier Henry Grenfel appears, she enjoys his company at the beginning, but as soon as she becomes aware of the affinity between March and Henry, she resents the intrusion of the young man into their lives. When March agrees to marry him, Banford succeeds in claiming her again. But the boy doesn't allow himself to be beaten, and Banford is accidentally killed. She shows in the story natural warmth and kindness, but she also displays anger and possessiveness.

Ellen March is the more robust of the two women who work on Bailey farm. She is the one strangely moved by the fox and spellbound by his casual arrogance and confidence. When Henry comes into their life, March recognizes him as the fox. She yields to the animal spell in Henry and accepts his marriage proposal. However, at the close of the story, she realizes that she cannot exert herself anymore either in action or in love.

Henry Grenfel is a young soldier who appears on the farm and examines the two women with sharp curiosity. He particularly likes March, not caring that she is older. Still, he feels himself master of her. He is sly and subtle, and he is able to suppress his youthful urgency in order to have March submit herself to him. He realizes very soon that March must be stalked and encompassed by superior cunning. Although he has won March by the story's closure, he knows that he has not possessed her completely.

The fox prowls about the farm stealing chickens. On only one occasion, before Henry shoots him, the fox is shown in a close encounter with March. They exchange glances and a kind of recognition takes place, to which the story owes its title. To March he becomes a representation of maleness and life itself. Henry Grenfel, a slyer hunter than the fox, kills him. ❁

Critical Views on
The Fox

IAN GREGOR ON "SUPRA-RATIONALITY"

[Ian Gregor is the author of *Great Web: The Form of Hardy's Major Fiction* (1974), and he is editor of *William Golding: A Critical Study* (1968) and *Imagined Worlds: Essays on Some English Novels and Novelists in Honour of John Butt* (1968). In this extract, taken from his essay "'The Fox': A Caveat," he discusses the connection between the fox and the boy.]

It is the fox which serves to focus March's 'blank musings' at the beginning of the tale. Her first encounter with him is completely unexpected:

> . . . his eyes were looking up. They met her eyes. And he knew her. She was spellbound . . . he looked into her eyes and her soul failed her.

The fox of course is the preparation for Henry, and it is through this kind of 'eye-recognition' that March's relationship with him is to be defined and communicated. The mode is all-pervasive:

> Suddenly he lifted his clouded blue eyes and unthinkingly looked straight into March's eyes. He was startled as well as she. He too recoiled a little. March felt the same sly taunting, knowing spark leap out of his eyes, as he turned his head aside, and fall into her soul, as it had fallen from the eyes of the fox.

> . . . her eyes were strangely clear, as he watched March, she turned her face aside . . . her consciousness dim.

> . . . she only looked at him with a wide, dark, vacant eye.

> One evening, sitting crocheting, March in her abstract intentness confuses the fox with the boy: March suddenly lifted her great dark eyes from her crocheting and saw him. She started, giving a little exclamation,

'There he is!' she said, involuntarily, as if terribly startled. It is not difficult to see why Lawrence is laying the stress in this way. The compulsive spontaneity of being that is found in the fox is to be found in the boy also, and it is to this that March is reacting. But there is nothing cognitive about this reaction, it is not a union of minds, but something supra-rational, an instinctive recognition of their mutual being. To convey this we have something like the use of the contemplative eye, the Wordsworthian use:

> Thou Eye among the blind,
> That, deaf and silent, read'st the Eternal Deep.

The kind of conjunction between the fox and the boy, and the boy and March, is a valuable one and is conveyed with ease and subtlety. But the conjunction begins to involve much more than this.

> To March he was the fox. Whether it was the thrusting forward of the head, or the glisten of fine, whitish hairs on the ruddy cheek bones, or the bright, keen eyes, that can never be said . . . but the boy was to her fox and she could not see him otherwise.

We have total identification—it is not simply the connection of 'eye-knowledge.'

> March lapsed into the odour of the fox . . . for the youth sent a faint, but distinct odour into the room, indefinable, like a wild creature.

'Like a wild creature,' that last phrase suggests how the significance of the boy extends out into the whole of animal creation—so that he breaks into 'a yap' of laughter, his face is 'cat-shaped,' his nose 'wrinkles like a puppy,' he 'yelps' with delight, his voice is like 'the merest touch of a cat's paw.' Now this kind of identification is so literal, so insistent, that the supra-rational element conveyed by 'the eyes' begins to be dominated by a sub-rational element which claims our attention by the stress on the totality of the identification between the boy's world and the animal world.

Terms like 'supra-rational' and 'sub-rational' are patently clumsy and inadequate here, but they serve to lay the emphasis we feel in reading, an emphasis which suggests a radical disturbance in the balance between the symbol and the reality. The fox is not so much assumed into the boy, as the boy becomes vulpine. Accompanying the animal presentation—the eyes, the features, the voice, the laugh— is a corresponding behaviour:

> He was a huntsman in spirit . . . and it was as a young hunter that he wanted to bring down March as his quarry.

> . . . even before you come in sight of your quarry, there is a strange battle, like mesmerism.

> He was off with the gun on every occasion. Nothing but the gun.

When he receives March's letter refusing him, his reactions are those of a trapped animal:

> He set his teeth, for a moment went almost pale, yellow round the eyes with fury. He said nothing and saw nothing and felt nothing, but a livid rage that was quite unreasoning. Balked! Balked again! Balked! He wanted the woman, he had fixed like doom upon having her. . . . With his teeth bitten together, his nose curiously slightly lifted, like some creature that is vicious, his eyes fixed and staring, he went through the morning's affairs, drunk with anger and suppression.

—Ian Gregor, "The Fox: A Caveat," *Essays in Criticism* 9 (1959): pp. 12–15.

KINGSLEY WIDMER ON THE EMOTIONAL TRIANGLE

[Kinsley Widmer is the author of *Defiant Desire: Some Dialectical Legacies of D. H. Lawrence* (1992), and *Edges of Extremity: Some Problems of Literary Modernism* (1980). In this extract taken from his book *The Art of Perversity: D. H. Lawrence's Shorter Fiction* (1962), he contemplates love. For Lawrence, Widmer claims, love is not only an agony but a leap over societal difficulties that brings forth no ultimate happiness or goodness.]

The Fox, a novella, has similar materials and motifs more elaborately developed, though the emotional triangle is not father-daughter-son but a man and a lesbian couple. In *The Fox*, utopian-yet-antiutopian Lawrence elaborates a negative analysis of the two girls in their "artsy-craftsy" return to the land, a small and isolated farm. The desire to create a private world makes all the more crucial the problem of vital personal relations; the two women are "losing hope" because they "seemed to live too much off themselves." Furthermore, in Lawrence's fictions homosexual relations defeat hope and love, perhaps because of a narcissism that lacks the creativeness of genuine polarity.

The masculine girl, March, robust in a forced way and "pinched as if in pain and misery," shows a "natural warmth." The more feminine Banford is genteel middle class, fearful, and dependent. March's emotional incompletion and oddity bring the symbolic forces of the unconscious into action, particularly in the form of her obsession with the malignant fox that preys upon the chicken farm. The demonic animal usurps March's consciousness: when he "looked into her eye," her "soul failed her"; "spellbound," she cannot shoot the marauder; his image fills her with dreams and reveries; "her heart beat to the fox, the fox." The red totemic image is likened to a devil, a serpent, a demon that seems malign at the conscious level but profoundly necessary to self-realization.

The demon lover, foretold by his fox totem, comes along to destroy the unvital harmony of the farm retreat. He is the soldier-grandson of the now dead former owner; and he is also the romantic outsider—the runaway youth, the exotic hero returned from Canada and Salonika, the strangely "knowing" and "wild creature," who, like Hadrian in *You Touched Me*, amorally desires both the property and the confrontation of the aging virgins. The lower-class hero is given symbolic portentousness by being made consubstantial with the demonic fox: they have a similar ruddiness, flaming smile, devilish qualities—the traditional marks of the satanic beast. And to March, Henry "was the fox . . . she could not see him otherwise."

But perhaps we should define more exactly what we mean when we speak of the fox as functioning "symbolically," since the word is used these days in so many different senses. For Lawrence, a symbol points neither to an ultimate reality of another order nor to a unique entity within apparent reality; a symbol is simply an ordinary fact showing transcendent subjective meaning. Thus when March loves Henry, his red face looks like that of the fox, but when March is negatively influenced by Banford's genteel and selfish ideas, Henry's red face (the fact does not change) becomes alien and inanimate—"a red chimney pot when looked at objectively" and "remotely." For Lawrence, there is only *one* reality, but the meaning of it depends on the relation of the person to it, and subjective immediacy is only reached by the removal of obstructing moral and social ideas. The fox itself is an actual object that has become a figure of representation or displacement for the most fundamental desires. Thus, the night of the youth's arrival March has a dream of the fox singing in the darkness, and when she goes to him he bites her and whisks his brush across her face so that "it seared and burned her mouth with a great pain." This dream of sexual anxiety parallels her responses when Henry actually kisses her and she feels burned and wounded. Her other dreams relating to the fox—such as covering the dead Banford in the firewood box with the fox's skin—show the same subjective significance and repeat the demonic pattern of sexuality and death, the fox and the fire, and desire and destruction. (Such metaphoric details as Banford—who insists on harassing the lovers—appearing with chrysanthemums, stand for unfulfilled death, as in *Odour of Chrysanthemums.*) Put in the form of an argument: the crucial subjectivity that constitutes individual fate or destiny cannot be realized in terms of rational statements or abstract codes; it must be realized as immediate sense experiences to which the individual has given full emotional response, since ultimate awareness is simply the fullest immediacy.

Thus, too, Henry's relationship to March does not become significant until she physically engages his awareness, and he sees her not as a personality but feels her as female "vulnerability." To accept such subjectivity is to have purpose and commitment, far more than through any "idea": "She was his heaven and hell on earth, and he would have none elsewhere." Henry's reaction to this burden of fate, this total engagement, is "rage" in which all lesser, objective, ethics become irrelevant.

Engaged by his demon, Henry frenziedly returns to the farm he has briefly left, where March is once again under Banford's repressive control and middle-class ideas. As with Lawrence's recurrent double heroines (*You Touched Me, Women in Love, Daughters of the Vicar,* etc.), the moralistic woman is the objective and rejecting side of the self and must be violently negated to allow vital completion. When the youth arrives, he finds Banford ineffectually chopping away at a dead tree; he takes over to destroy the dead past, and, impelled by his love commitment, he carries out a destructive ritual. With sly propriety, he warns Banford that the tree may hit her. Because he said it, she refuses to move—as Henry expected—and he intentionally cuts the tree down in such a way as to kill her.

As with the other symbolic procedures in the story, the killing appears actual as well as symbolic. Such is the harshness of destiny and the perversity of love. Banford dead, March is emotionally free and, with the romantic ordeal completed, marries Henry at Christmas. When the ritualistic sanction of murder for the fulfillment of life destiny occurs in *Sons and Lovers* it is perhaps less clear, because the mother is dying anyway and because Paul Morel has been developed as an exceptional and artistic youth. But in *The Fox*, and similar works, the violation of morality and human life dramatically develops in terms of a simple, nonintellectual, and nonartistic, hero. The implication remains that not only the unique hero but Everyman must transcend morality to achieve love and destiny.

—Kingsley Widmer, *The Art of Perversity: D. H. Lawrence's Shorter Fiction.* (Seattle: University of Washington Press, 1962): pp. 59–62.

R. E. PRITCHARD ON LAWRENCE'S IDEAL

[In this extract taken from his book on Lawrence, R. E. Pritchard discusses briefly the difference between the first and final versions of the story.]

The struggle against feminine inhibition appears in the three long tales of this period—'The Fox,' 'The Captain's Doll,' and 'The Ladybird.' The first of these was originally written about the same time as 'You Touched Me' and was a variation on that theme, of the lower-class younger man enforcing the submission of one of two women. Here two women, Banford and March, are in escape from society on a remote chicken-farm, engaged in a sterile lesbian relationship. Banford is white, frail and nervous (the social, selfconscious self) while March, in trousers, is the stronger passionate being; her repressed sexual desires appear in her obsession with a thieving fox, the precursor of the young man (Lawrence's modulation between the realistic and symbolic levels is very well done here). The difference between the first and the final version, which has much greater intensity and savagery (indicating perhaps Lawrence's own more desperate situation) is revealed by indicating what incidents are missing from the first version. It does not show the young man assuming the fox's power by killing and crucifying it; nor March's repeated caresses of the dead fox's (phallic) brush, even getting blood on her hand, like Gudrun; nor the young man's killing of Banford, employing her own feminine, perverse resistance, so that the dead tree of her withered passional self falls on her, smashing her head; while, at the end, instead of a simple anticipation of new life, Lawrence eventually added a passage implicitly admitting the impossibility of attaining the ideal. There he suggests that the ideal is like death, and to strain for it perverse, because at the centre of (his own?) being was something fearful, horrible, essentially null:

> The more you reached after the fatal flower of happiness, which trembles so blue and lovely in a crevice just beyond your grasp, the more fearfully you become aware of the ghastly gulf of the precipice below you, into which you will immediately plunge, as into the bottomless pit, if you reach any further. You pluck flower after flower—it is never *the* flower. The flower itself—its calyx is a horrible gulf, it is the bottomless pit.

Lawrence's ideal is, he senses, regressive and self-destructive: within the flower, associated with spontaneity and maleness (perhaps its blueness links it with his mother, also) is the gulf, the pit of unthinkable and terrifying desires. In Alvina Houghton, he had expressed even greater horror at the consequences of abandonment to a lower male being of intense sexuality.

'*The Fox* belongs more to the old world' wrote Lawrence, expressing the view that the other two tales were more exploratory; certainly in them the fantasy becomes more extreme.

—R. E. Pritchard, *D. H. Lawrence: Body of Darkness* (Pittsburgh: University of Pittsburgh Press, 1971): pp. 140–41.

E. F. Shields on Broken Vision

[In this extract taken from his essay "Broken Vision in Lawrence's 'The Fox,'" E. F. Shields reflects on the "ironic distance" of the narrator.]

⟨T⟩he story has been told by a perceptive, intelligent narrator who has been able to present the emotional conflicts of the characters in such a way that the reader understands the characters far better than they understand themselves. In other words, the narrator has been able to keep what we might call an "ironic distance" from the characters; although various details, such as the sterility of the chicken farm, are used to weight the story against March and Banford's essay in female self-sufficiency, the narrator never associates himself with the ignorance or blindness of the characters. But with the death of Banford a split occurs in the narrator: Lawrence the creative artist who has presented the story through the persona of the narrator now comes in conflict with Lawrence the philosopher and prophet. The narrator, who on the surface remains the same, is actually divided into two persons. As Lawrence the prophet intrudes, a different and artistically less perceptive narrative voice appears.

Consequently, we find the narrator "taken in" by Banford's murder. While it is understandable that Henry should view Banford's death as a desirable means to an end, it is inconceivable that the perceptive narrator of the first part should view the action in the same light. Henry sees Banford as the source of his problems; thus, for him, the solution is simple. But it is obvious to the reader that Henry has oversimplified and misunderstood the problem. Banford is not the cause of March's latent Lesbianism; she is merely the object. To eliminate Banford is not to eliminate the source of the problem. The source is within March herself. Yet, in describing the killing, the narrator accepts the distorted and obviously inadequate view of Henry: "The inner necessity of his life was fulfilling itself, it was he who was to live. The thorn was drawn out of his bowels." There is no indication on the part of the narrator that Henry's triumphant exultation is unjustified. Instead, the narrator tends to associate his own view with that of Henry and to see the act as both necessary and good.

What has happened here is quite subtle. Lawrence, the creative artist who intuitively understands the emotions of his characters, realizes that Henry might well deliberately bring about Banford's death; at the same time, Lawrence the reflective thinker and social commentator feels that in certain circumstances it is necessary to commit murder in order to allow the forces of life to triumph over the forces of death. In "The Fox," the second Lawrence sees the situation developed by the first Lawrence as an illustration of his idea; consequently, there is a breakdown in narrative consistency as the second Lawrence so intrudes on the story as to force the narrator to lose his ironic distance and identify with Henry's views. Whereas up to the murder, both the reader and the narrator have understood the situation better than the characters, with the murder the reader is forced to separate from the narrator because he now sees the event more clearly than the narrator.

Throughout the rest of the story, there is a struggle for control between Lawrence the artist and Lawrence the thinker—both making use of the same narrator. Lawrence the thinker wants to solve the problem through the imposition of a Laurentian thesis; Lawrence the artist is far too honest to allow this fakery—he wants to resolve the problem through the terms presented in the story itself; he realizes that March will not be converted with a flash of lightning or a stroke of the axe. Because of this conflict, because some sections are so right while others are so wrong, some critics can see the ending as an appropriate and organic development of the story while others can see it is a piece of tacked-on Laurentian propaganda. In reality, it is neither and yet both. The artist does not completely give over the ending to the thinker, but at the same time he is not completely in control.

We can see this vacillation clearly in the story. Immediately after Banford's death, March confronts Henry: "She looked up at him with tears running from her eyes, a senseless look of helplessness and submission. So she gazed on him as if sightless, yet looking up to him. She would never leave him again. He had won her. And he knew it and was glad, because he wanted her for his life. His life must have her. And now he had won her. It was what his life must have." Everything, apparently, is settled. But Lawrence the artist, working on an emotional level, understanding the real pressures and drives within March, knows that the murder really hasn't solved anything. Thus, we find the narrator acknowledging this fact, with what is almost a verbal quibble: "But if he had won her, he had not yet got her." The perceptive narrator is back; he sees the essential futility of the murder and, in effect, renounces the murder as ineffective. Even without Banford, March retains her essential desire to have someone dependent on her. Instead of responding joyfully—she has gained Henry—she becomes depressed, feeling she has lost something she wanted and needed; her soul "droops." What she has lost, of course, is her relationship with a female; whatever forces first led her into her involvement with Banford are still there; they have not been eliminated or supplanted by Henry since Henry basically fulfills a different type of need. As artist, Lawrence understands that the elimination of Banford creates a void in March's life which cannot be filled by Henry; the problem then is to find some resolution, and once more the artist is hard pressed in his attempts to work out the problems he has depicted. As a result, we find Lawrence the thinker quickly stepping in to explain the problem: March's concept of love is wrong—she insists on exerting herself, on attempting to take the male's active role. Being a woman, she should "be submerged under the surface of love."

—E. F. Shields, "Broken Vision in Lawrence's 'The Fox,'" *Studies in Short Fiction* 9, no. 4 (Fall 1972): 356–58.

Albert J. Devlin on How to Read *The Fox*

[Albert J. Devlin is a professor of English Literature at the University of Missouri-Columbia. He has written widely on Southern American literature. His most recent work is *Eudora Welty's Chronicle: A Story of Mississippi Life*. In this extract he discusses the composition of *The Fox*.]

When *The Fox* was published in March 1923 in collection with *The Ladybird* and *The Captain's Doll*, this novella had been extended to nearly three times the length of the original story. The original story ended with Henry Grenfel's abrupt proposal of marriage to March, her mystical acceptance, Banford's muted dismay, and then the factual report of marriage followed by Henry's departure 'in ten days['] time.' The 'long tail' that Lawrence attached to *The Fox* in 1921 begins with the above proposal scene, but Nellie March is now granted resistance to the 'curious power' of Henry's voice, and the scene itself dissolves inconclusively when Jill Banford calls from the house, "'Are you out there?'" Thereafter the mutual struggle of Henry, March and Banford is expanded and intensified until it concludes with the death of Banford. On 16 February 1918, Lawrence wrote gloomily to Mark Gertler about the treachery of modern history: 'Nowadays one can do nothing but glance behind to see who now is creeping up to do something horrible to the back of one's neck.' Lawrence's lament seems to anticipate with no little irony of reversal the fate ordained for 'the Banford,' an exemplar of decadent modernity. Henry Grenfel 'gave two swift, flashing blows, in immediate succession. . . . No one heard the strange little cry which the Banford gave as the dark end of the bough swooped down, down on her. No one saw her crouch a little and receive the blow on the back of the neck.'

As this description indicates, *The Fox* was not the product of one sustained creative endeavour. Instead, its composition was spread over three years that were tumultuous even by Lawrence's standards. Lawrence left England on 14 November 1919. Thereafter, 'the spirit of pilgrimage by which he lived' (the phrasing is L. D. Clark's) drew Lawrence south to Italy, specifically to Florence, Rome and Capri, before he and Frieda settled in March 1920 at the Villa Fontana Vecchia in Taormina. But even the relative stability of their two-year residence in Sicily was upset by wandering to Syracuse, Malta and Sardinia, and, more distantly, to Italy, Germany and Austria. Lawrence's travel between 1919 and 1921 undoubtedly broadened his range of experience and heightened his normally avid response to new people and places, further enriching the personal and cultural matrix of *The Fox*. Its growth during this period from an 'odd and amusing' tale into one that Lawrence thought 'so modern, so new,' has not, however, been treated carefully by critics, especially by those who take formalistic exception to Lawrence's work. This transformation merits careful study because it contains implicit evidence of Lawrence's artistic integrity and control. As noted above, *England, My England, The Lost Girl* and *Aaron's Rod* can best guide this developmental study of thematic issues which appear and mature in the 'strange and fiery' course of *The Fox*. ⟨. . .⟩

The first draft of *The Fox* is a unique, irrecoverable instance of temperament, circumstance, and execution. But while its appearance in December 1918 may not have been predictable, Lawrence's story nonetheless speaks in one rhythm with the adjoining stories of *England, My England* and betrays the same formative concerns and hopes engendered by the First World War. The links between the first draft of *The Fox* and the stories of *England, My England* need only brief enumeration here. The argument of the title story, that the First World War marks the end of old England and forecasts a time of 'ugly disintegration,' is ratified by the ironic pastoral of Bailey Farm—the hens do not lay, a heifer 'refused absolutely' to be corralled, and the landscape is uniformly 'black' when winter comes in Berkshire. In addition, wartime restraints on hunting have increased the 'evil' of the fox until he becomes 'a demon,' plundering 'the hens under the very noses of March and Banford.' As Nellie March trudges through this ironic version of pastoral, she reveals a symptomatic disquietude that aligns her conceptually with the troubled women of *England, My England*. Her 'consciousness was, as it were, held back' from vital contact with the unknown self. The arrival of Henry Grenfel fulfils the prophecy of renewal conveyed by March's earlier encounter with the fox, and thus begins 'the great creative process' of love that Lawrence foresaw. Banford's resistance to this creativity is scarcely developed in the first draft of *The Fox*, although her incipient role as Magna Mater to Henry evokes the deranged sexuality of *England, My England*. Had Lawrence not recognised the potential of his material, the 'odd and amusing' tale that he completed in 1918 might have been added to *England, My England*, for their main lines of cultural conception and artistic rendering are nearly congruent. Neither is intelligible apart from its source in England's precipitous fall into the First World War and Lawrence's hope for 'resurrection.' This early history of *The Fox* partially answers the opening question, but a more satisfactory answer must await examination of Lawrence's motives in revising a relatively untroubled story of 'youthful love.' How to read the expanded version of *The Fox* of 1921 that Lawrence found 'so modern, so new,' depends upon further study conducted along intertextual lines. Such criticism will cause us to reflect upon Lawrence's underlying integrity of motive and to recognise his true achievement of ends in *The Fox*.

The elements of complication that give *The Fox* its 'strange and fiery' momentum were ordained by Lawrence's personal experience and tested aesthetically in *The Lost Girl* (1920) and *Aaron's Rod* (1922). For Lawrence, the doctrine of 'resurrection' simply means to keep vital company with the indwelling godhead. As he explained to Gordon Campbell in September 1914, 'we want to realise the tremendous *non-human* quality of life—

it is wonderful. It is not the emotions, nor the personal feelings and attachments, that matter. These are all only expressive, and expression has become mechanical. Behind us all are the tremendous unknown forces of life, coming unseen and unperceived as out of the desert to the Egyptians, and driving us, forcing us, destroying us if we do not submit to be swept away.

—Albert J. Devlin, "The 'Strange and Fiery' Course of *The Fox:* D. H. Lawrence's Aesthetic of Composition and Revision," in *The Spirit of D. H. Lawrence: Centenary Studies,* edited by Gāmini Salgādo and G. K. Das. (Totowa, N.J.: Barnes & Noble Books, 1988): pp. 77–78, 81–82.

Plot Summary of
"The Captain's Doll"

"The Captain's Doll" is the first of the three long tales Lawrence wrote in the winter of 1920–21. The story is loosely based on "The Mortal Coil," which was omitted from the *England, My England* volume. On November 2, 1920, Lawrence wrote a letter to his artist friend Earl Brewster about his literary projects: "I suddenly wrote a very funny long story called "The Captain's Doll"—which I haven't finished yet. But I have just got it high up in the mountains of the Tyrol, and do not quite know how to get it down without breaking its neck." Four days later, the finale of the story was written.

The story begins in a town in Allied-occupied Germany after the First World War. The precise location is not defined, but it could be Cologne, which British troops occupied between December 1918 and January 1926. Later, the setting moves to Munich, and then to Kaprun on a lake in the Austrian Tyrol.

The first movement of the story opens with a dialogue in German between Mitchka (Baroness Annamaria von Prielau-Carolath) and Hannele (Countess Johanna zu Rassentlow). We are taken into Hannele's apartment where she is making a doll of a Scotch soldier in tight-fitting tartan trams. Mitchka wanders around, and as she observes the room, the reader gets the first glimpse of its owner, Captain Hepburn, who shares the attic space with Hannele. The room holds tobacco and pipes on a little tray, two guns on a bracket, and two telescopes, one mounted on a stand near the window. Mitchka's remark on the Captain—"He is at a closed end. I don't know where I can get to with him, Aren't you afraid of him, too Hannele? Ach, like a closed road"—is meant to intrigue the reader.

As the subtle and succinct dialogue unfolds, we gain a sense of the Captain and his relationship with Hannele. Alexander Hepburn has had a love affair with Hannele, according to the rumors, but now that he is on leave for a month, he might have to go home to his wife of seventeen years. Although Hannele is distressed by his calm acceptance of the situation, she feels helpless in his presence. She has to struggle with her soul.

> When he put his hand again on her cheek, softly, with the most extraordinary soft half-touch, as a kitten's paw sometimes touches

one, like a fluff of living air, then, if it had not been for the magic of that almost indiscernible caress of his hand, she would have stiffened herself and drawn away and told him she could have nothing to do with him, while he was so half-hearted and unsatisfactory. She wanted to tell him these things. But when she began he answered invariably in the same soft, straying voice, that seemed to spin gossamer threads over her, so that she could neither think nor act nor even feel distinctly. Her soul groaned rebelliously in her.

The first movement of the tale ends, leaving the reader entangled in the characters' affections. Both the captain and Hannele have won their case with the reader.

Countess zu Rassentlow lives as a refugee in a studio on one of the main streets. She and Mitchka make dolls and embroidered cushions for a living. When Hepburn's wife Evangeline arrives unexpectedly from England to regain possession of her husband, she visits the store, without revealing her identity, and sees the mannikin doll of her husband. Subsequently, when Hannele realizes her identity, Evangeline offers to buy the doll. Wrongly suspicious of Mitchka, she threatens to have them both removed by the authorities if they do not cooperate. Lawrence describes her confusion.

> So she started afresh, trying to keep a tight hold on the tail of that all-too-evanescent magic of his. Dear, it slipped so quickly into disillusion. Nevertheless. If it had existed it did exist. And if did exist, it was worth having. You could call it an illusion if you liked. But an illusion which is a real experience is worth having. Perhaps this disillusion was a greater illusion than the illusion itself. Perhaps all this disillusion of the little lady and the husband of the little lady was falser that the illusion and magic of those few evenings. Perhaps the long disillusion of life is falser than the brief moments of real illusion.

Before the lady is able to carry out her dire threat, she accidentally falls out of her hotel room window and is killed. Hepburn is overwhelmed. He decides he has to withdraw not only from his relationship with Hannele but from all other people as well. He feels somehow that the emotional flow between him and all people has been broken, so he returns to England to settle his affairs with his two children; he also obtains his discharge from the army. Hannele, having seen that Hepburn played the puppet for his wife, sells the doll and departs.

After a year has passed, Hepburn, who is not a man to live alone, begins his search for Hannele. She does not represent, in the narrator's words, "rosy love" to him but rather "a hard destiny." In Munich, he sees the doll in a shop window and is angered by it. When, after a week or so, he finds that the doll has been sold again, he buys a surreal still-life painting that shows the doll together with sunflowers and poached eggs.

Lawrence never lets the symbol usurp the action. His novella is centered on the man, not the doll, as Widmer rightly points out: "He does not use symbol as the reality, nor even as the perception of reality, but simply as an analogy of the subjective problem of the hero."

Hepburn reads in the local newspaper of Countess zu Rassentlow's engagement to Herr Regeirungsrat von Poldi, at Kaprun, in the Tyrol. He sets off at once to Austria.

In the final long section of the tale, Lawrence takes the captain and Hannele on a holiday excursion to a glacier. The story breaks into one of Lawrence's classic fights that represent the opposing visions on love and marriage; the characters are also caught between two worlds. On the one hand is a crowd "in a frenzy to be happy or to be thrilled," while on the other hand lies the cold, cold, dangerous glacier. Again and again, we feel Lawrence's astonishing gift for the vibrancy of natural imagery:

> It seems as if the ice breathed here. The wonder, the terror, and the bitterness of it. Never a warm leaf to unfold, never a gesture of life to give off. A world sufficient unto itself in lifelessness, all this ice.

The dialogue urges us to see the quarrel as raising rather than settling issues. Hepburn wants marriage but not love, he wants a woman to honor and obey him, a sort of patient Griseldis (as in Boccaccio); meanwhile, Hannele insists that if you love, then everything is there—the whole lot: your honor and obedience and everything. Hepburn plans to go to East Africa ("woman or no woman, I'm going to do that") and to write a book on the moon.

Delaying the closure as long as possible, Lawrence ends the story with Hannele accepting the kind of marriage he is proposing ("To be a wife—and to be loved and cherished as a wife—not as a flirting woman."), though the experienced reader cannot be sure that this marriage will be unequivocally on Hepburn's own terms. ❈

List of Characters in
"The Captain's Doll"

Hannele (Countess Johanna zu Rassentlow) is a fair woman with soft, dark blonde hair, fine skin, and a certain glow of life about her. She is a refugee in defeated Germany, forced to work for her living. She makes and sells dolls and is very successful. Her best work is the model of her lover, Captain Hepburn. She can't help being in love with him, although she is at the same time bitter about their relationship, since he is so ineffectual and indecisive. When, after the death of his wife, he disappears from her life, she gets engaged to Herr Poldi, only to give him up when the Captain shows up a year later.

Captain Alexander Hepburn is a tall, Scottish captain with dark eyes and dark hair. When his superiors are alerted to his affair with Hannele, they advise him to leave for England. He often has an incomprehensible, gargoyle-like smile on his face. After a year of solitude, he feels a great need to be with someone and begins his search for Hannele. He proposes to her not because he longs for love, but because he wants her respect and obedience. She half yields, but he remains unyielding.

Mrs. Evangeline Hepburn is the wife of Captain Hepburn. She has a tiny figure, bright eyes, and a middle-class voice. She erroneously thinks that Mitchka is her husband's lover and confides that to Hannele. She demands the doll from Hannele and issues the ultimatum that she will have Hannele and Mitchka removed by military authorities if they do not cooperate. She mysteriously falls from the hotel room window and is killed.

Mitchka (Baroness Annamaria von Prielau-Carolath) is a friend and partner of Hannele. The Captain's wife mistakes her for his lover. When Hepburn tries to find Hannele, he learns that Mitchka was shot dead in a riot in Salzburg.

Herr Regierungsrat von Poldi is about 50 years old, and he is the local governor in the Tyrol district and fiancé to Hannele. His carelessness and *grande geste* deeply impresses Hannele. However, he becomes completely insignificant to her when Captain Hepburn turns up again. ❀

Critical Views on
"The Captain's Doll"

LEO GURKO ON THE LIBERATION PROCESS

[Leo Gurko is the author of *Ernest Hemingway and the Pursuit of Heroism* (1968), *Thomas Wolfe: Beyond the Romantic Ego* (1975), and *Joseph Conrad, Giant in Exile* (1979). In this excerpt taken from his essay on Lawrence's collection of short stories, he discusses the emblem motif that underlines Lawrence's story.]

"The Captain's Doll," with its sense of deliberate comedy, is especially resistant to definition by traditional romance, whether folk or myth. We are encouraged to look more intently within the stories themselves for clues to their collective meaning.

The element first encountered is the titles, each containing a symbol for a figure within. The ladybird or scarab is the emblem for the Count, the fox for Henry, the doll for the captain. These emblem images are embodiments of some significant quality in the man, but because they represent only the one quality, they are caricatures. They are, in effect, to use one of Lawrence's favorite terms, *reductions* of the men. We see the men in them clearly enough, but in a shrunken way. The problem for each—the problem of the stories—is how to be freed from the emblem into themselves, how to escape from their imprisonment as caricatures and regain their living wholeness.

The liberation process is particularly marked in "The Captain's Doll." The Countess makes a doll of her Scottish lover as a sign of her exasperation with him. The doll is a perfect physical likeness, down to the tight-fitting tartan trews. Seeing it for the first time, the Captain says, "You've got me." But the point of course is that she hasn't got him. All that she has caught of him is his physical self, down to his straight, handsome legs mentioned several times during the course of the story. The visible part of him is all she can take hold of; the invisible side of him—vague, non-thinking, gazing at her with "that other, unseeing look"—eludes her. She is fascinated by it, but cannot pin it down, and in her frustration imprisons in the doll the part of him that she can pin down. The doll expresses her relationship with the Captain when the story opens; it has been sexually satisfactory and emotionally baffling. As long as the doll stands between them, their relationship cannot progress.

The Captain is a doll not only to the Countess but also to his wife. With her "lardy-dardy middle-class English," her sense of ownership and her obsessively feminine determination "to protect our men," Mrs. Hepburn is triumphantly characterized. On their wedding night, she extracted from her husband a promise, delivered on his knees, to love and adore her. This suppliant position confirms his function as her doll, a possessed subservient object that feeds her emotionally. Even when he ceases to "love" and "adore" her, he continues, willingly and calmly, to make love to her—a fact that shocks the Countess. Paradoxically, she finds it hard to believe that the man of whom she has made a doll has been one for eighteen years to another woman.

With the wife's death, the Captain is freed from his bondage to her. He repudiates the love-adoration posture and sets off in pursuit of the Countess in search of another kind of relationship. But first he must get rid of the doll. He finds it staring at him uncannily in a Munich shop window, and later as part of a fashionable still-life canvas, surrounded by two sun-flowers in a glass jar and a poached egg on toast. The doll disappears, but he buys the still-life, turns it over to the Countess when he finds her, and in the end, when a new and unexpected union between them is created, she burns the painting as a sign that the Captain's phase as a doll is over and his phase as a man has begun. ⟨. . .⟩

The emblem motif underlines Lawrence's conviction that modern life tends to shrink human beings into objects and abstractions, and that it is the mission of art to reverse the process, to restore men to their original individuality and wholeness.

But while this motif powerfully affects the men in these stories, it does not take the women into account. Yet their fate depends on the equilibrium established with the men. This equilibrium had been set forth as a theory not long before by Birkin in *Women in Love*, and emerges as one of the binding elements in these tales at the beginning of the '20's. The Countess is too masculine and "free" at the start of the "The Captain's Doll." Her excessive independence, assertiveness, and desire to get hold of the Captain—his vagueness irritates and disorients her—are as much her response to the unsettled times as to the compulsions of her own nature. The Captain's elusiveness is due to his married subservience. He has yielded too much of himself to his wife. Not until she dies can his balance be regained and can he be free to create a new relationship with the Countess. The equilibrium they finally establish is achieved not through harmony, friendly negotiations, and prudent adjustments, but through argument, angry dialectic, and a period of prolonged tension. They are deeply attracted to one another, but the ground through which they must pass is a minefield of resentments, demands, ultimatums, and mutual rage. The quarrel over the words in the marriage ceremony is characteristic of these collisions. He wants her not to love but to honor and obey him. She is anxious to love him, but is not prepared to honor and obey. It is an outrage, she feels, for an emancipated woman thus to humble herself before a man. So, they quarrel, argue, and drive at each other. She finally gives way, grudgingly, reluctantly, not at all in the state of passive radiance typical of the traditional heroine. The equilibrium they reach is an equilibrium of tension. Their opposing male and female selves do work out an understanding, but it is an uneasy truce that prevails, not a stabilized peace.

—Leo Gurko, "D. H. Lawrence's Greatest Collection of Stories—What Holds It Together," *Modern Fiction Studies* 18, no. 2 (Summer 1972): pp. 175–78.

F. R. Leavis on Individuality and Love as Opposing Forces

[F. R. Leavis (1895–1978) was founder of the review *Scrutiny*, Fellow and Director of English Studies at Downing College, Cambridge, and University Reader in English. He achieved worldwide fame in his lifetime as teacher, critic, lecturer, and writer. Among his publications are *New Bearings in English Poetry* (1932), *Revaluation* (1936), *The Great Tradition* (1948), *Anna Karenina and Other Essays* (1967), *Dickens the Novelist* (1970; with his wife Q. D. Leavis), and *The Critic as Anti-Philosopher* (1982). In this extract taken from his book *Thought, Words and Creativity: Art and Thought in Lawrence* (1976), he discusses the problem of individuality and love that faces the Captain and Hannelle in "The Captain's Doll."]

I think that my reader will do well to read along with 'The Captain's Doll' an expository essay of Lawrence's own: '. . . Love was once a Little Boy' (*Reflections on the Death of a Porcupine* in which it appeared is included in *Phoenix II*). It serves to emphasize the fact that the tale is amply enough invested with a complexity of its own, and is full of very relevant felicities. It is enough at the moment to quote one of them:

> Hate is not the opposite of love. The real opposite of love is individuality. We live in the age of individuality, we call ourselves the servants of love. That is to say, we enact a perpetual paradox. ⟨. . .⟩

We have here what might be said to be a general statement of the problem that faces the Captain and Hannele in 'The Captain's Doll.' The evoking of the problem as, in its formidable changing concreteness, it enacts itself between them (each, of course, feeling it in his or her own distinctive way) is marvellously done, the doing depending largely on Lawrence's genius for dramatic dialogue. ⟨. . .⟩

What both Hannele and Mitchka in the opening of the tale are impressed by is the potent individuality of the Captain. The very first paragraph intimates that the making of the doll must involve taking liberties: 'She was doing something to the knee of the mannikin, so that the poor little gentleman flourished head downwards with arms widely tossed out.' But the essential paradox entails a conscious emphasis on the impressive distinction:

> The face was beautifully modelled, and a wonderful portrait, dark-skinned, with a little, close-cut, dark moustache, and wide-open dark eyes, and that air of aloofness and perfect diffidence which marks an officer and a gentleman.

It is Mitchka who, all innocently, registers the inescapable element of irony:

> Exactly him. Just as finished as he is. Just as complete. He is just like that: finished off.

'Exactly him,' 'finished,' 'complete,' 'finished off'—at our first introduction to the doll we are not allowed to miss the paradox. It is significant that Hannele, we are soon to be told, should ask herself why she had made it. She had made it, of course, with her artist's talent as a tribute to his individuality. But if life is individuality, the life-flow in the Captain is very strong; his presence is 'incalculable.' The unknown enters with life freely at the well-head, and her sense of that is what makes him irresistible to Hannele. The visual effects that are possible in the most wonderfully life-like doll can't—in spite of the 'wide-open dark eyes'—render what makes the incalculable life in him affect her so with vitalizing wonder.

> Hannele was most uneasy because she seemed to have forgotten him in the three days whilst he had been away. He seemed to have disappeared out of her.

But when she heard his voice on the stairs, she 'knew there *was* something there.'

We are also told—told at the same time—that 'she was afraid again.' And we have a pointer here to the underlying significance of the uneasiness, the self-suspicion, implicit in her asking herself why she had made the doll. You know where you are with what is 'finished off.' Hannele of course was incapable of willing consciously to suppress the formidable mystery, the male incalculableness, she found so impressive in the Captain. Is it not there in the doll? It's there!—the wide-open dark eyes most certainly *are* there. But she has made a doll of him—as every woman, Alexander tells her, is ready to make a doll of her man. And when the Captain's doll becomes a figure in Theodor Worpswede's Still-leben the stillness of the unliving is emphasized. Hannele, when she turned her face from the picture 'as a cat turns its nose away from a lighted cigarette,' betrayed an uneasy sense that she deserved to be held, in some unspecified way, at least suspect. As for Alexander's bracketing her with her female opposite, his wife, who made no literal dolls, it had its point. The little lady did indeed make a metaphorical doll of her husband, which in denying him the strong individuality as a male that characterizes him, merely served her stupid, petty and confident ego. Hannele (like Ursula) was *not* stupid, and the shockingly gross instance, of which the bearing ('offensively' insisted on) was plain, certainly told in the sudden surrender at the close—the tacit withdrawal of her refusal to see the validity of Alexander's insistence on the confusions engendered by the word 'love' and, positively, on the conditions of a permanent union.

Hannele certainly knows that he loves her, and he himself actually uses in a positive way the word 'love' on the penultimate page:

> 'Well,' he said slowly, 'she'll be my wife, and I shall treat her as such. If the marriage service says love and cherish—well, in that sense I shall do so.'
> 'Oh!' cried Hannele. 'What, *love* her? Actually love the poor thing?'
> 'Not in that sense of the word, no. I shan't adore her or be in love with her. But she'll be my wife, and I shall love and cherish her as such.'
> 'Just because she's your wife. Not because she's herself. Ghastly fate for any miserable woman,' said Hannele.
> 'I don't think so. I think it's her highest fate.'
> 'To be your wife?'
> 'To be a wife—and to be loved and shielded as a wife—not as a flirting woman.'

In my one-volume collection of the tales there are thirty-six lines left before the end of 'The Captain's Doll.' Hannele is a spirited woman, and even though she loves Alexander and profoundly (we see) trusts him, we wonder how the tale is to be brought to an end both inevitable in terms of the thought and compellingly natural. We find that the answer exemplifies the advantage, if you are a great novelist and D. H. Lawrence, of tackling a major human theme that challenges basic thought in a—*as a*—*nouvelle*.

> As they were rowing in silence over the lake, he said: 'I shall leave tomorrow.'
> She made no answer. She sat and watched the lights of the villa draw near. And then she said: 'I'll come to Africa with you. But I won't promise to honour and obey you.'
> 'I don't want you otherwise,' he said, very quietly. The boat was drifting to the little landing stage. Hannele's friends were hallooing to her from the balcony.
> 'Hallo!' she cried. 'Ja. Da bin ich. Ja, 's war wunderschön.'
> Then to him she said:
> 'You'll come in?'
> 'No,' he said, 'I'll row straight back.'

From the villa they were running down the steps to meet Hannele.

'But won't you have me even if I love you?' she asked him.

'You must promise the other,' he said. 'It comes in the marriage service.'

'Hat's geregnet? Wie war das Wetter? Warst du auf dem Gletscher?' cried the voices from the garden.

'Nein—kein Regen. Wunderschön! Ja, er war ganz auf dem Gletscher,' cried Hannele in reply. And to him, *sotto voce*:

'Don't be a solemn ass. Do come in.'

'No,' he said, 'I don't want to come in.'

'Do you want to go away tomorrow? Go, if you *do*. But anyway, I won't say it *before* the marriage service. I needn't, need I?'

She stepped from the boat on to the plank.

'Oh,' she said, turning round, 'give me that picture, please, will you? I want to burn it.'

There are four further lines to leave us assured that this *is* the quietly matter-of-fact but clinching inevitable end and upshot—a wholly satisfying resolution. Hannele, intelligent as she is, couldn't have brought her pride and habit to allow such a change to be so easy—change to recognizing Alexander's good sense—but for the voices shouting their questions from the garden, and the answers coming so naturally from her: 'Nein, kein Regen. Wunderschön! Ja, er war ganz auf dem Gletscher.' The implication of the tone has a supporting context. Such an answer confirms her friends' sense, and in confirming it confirms her own, that the relations between her and Alexander which make the joint excursion to the glacier so natural seem to point to the pair's becoming—the pair they essentially are or are meant to be—formally and really husband and wife.

And actually the friction between them and their manner of conveying it imply that they matter to one another as profoundly as a man and a woman can. They are intimate with a reality far more real than the intimacy of a pair of lovers intoxicated with the passion of adoring love. The running altercation between them is that of a man and a woman who essentially *want* to justify their feeling that, between them, they have the qualities that might go to form a permanent union of the right kind. The trouble of course is that they differ as to what the right kind is. Alexander is equally with Birkin confronted by the reflected image of the moon which always re-forms when he has done his best to shatter and disperse it.

After a moment's silence she [Ursula] replied:

'But how can I, you don't love me! You only want your own ends. You don't want to serve me, and yet you want me to serve you. It is so one-sided!'

The firmness of Hannele's refusal is of the same order, and expresses itself in the same way, though it is undermined by incipient intuition:

But because he gave himself away, she forgave him. And the strange passion of his, that gave out incomprehensible flashes, *was* rather fascinating to her. She felt just a tiny bit sorry for him. But she wasn't going to be bullied by him. She wasn't going to give in to him and his black passion. No, never. For love on equal terms she was quite ready. She only waited for him to offer it.

She waited in vain. What she called 'love on equal terms' went with the self-ignorance that made her ask uneasily *what* had moved her to make the doll of Alexander. Both the doll and the demand for 'love on equal terms' are expressions of the female ego: the flatteringness of the doll and the plausibility of the demand are specious; they cover resentment at the male strength that went with the mystery in Alexander—the profound vital maleness that Hannele, in her complex reaction, so admired in him and that made her at the root of herself, for all his disconcertingness, trust him as she did. She came (but pulled up) to the brink of marrying the Herr Regierungsrat because his way of kissing her hand made her feel 'like a queen in exile.' But when the Captain reappears her profounder being at once decides for *him*. This is what gives its distinctive meaning to the glacier-excursion *with one another*—which has for end of the enacted drama the accordant and significant outcome. The friction and running altercation confirm in him the lesson of the 'love'-marriage with the little lady; it is for the man in especial to cultivate his singleness and to devote himself to some creative purpose that the deeper, the non-ego promptings of his individuality impel him to, or there will be no prosperous final union.

Every human sameness is different; it couldn't occur to Birkin to talk of the marriage service or to enjoin Ursula to honour and obey. But the appropriateness of such terms and such talk when Alexander is concerned to bring home to Hannele the kind of finality he has in mind is triumphantly vindicated by 'The Captain's Doll.' The easy succession of her utterances is significant:

'Ja, er war ganz auf dem Gletscher,' cried Hannele in reply. And to him, *sotto voce*: 'Don't be a solemn ass. Do come in.'

She is merely showing how completely she has come to share his attitude and his sense of things, and that Hannele married won't be the less Hannele.

The tale ends on this sentence: 'He pulled back quickly into the darkness.' Such a close prompts us to observe that the darkness in Alexander is always close at hand and very accessible; that is for him a condition of the deep responsibility that distinguishes him—and so neither for this darkness has Hannele anything to fear. She knows it.

It is perhaps proper to insist after such an exercise, of which I am all too conscious of the clumsiness, that I have not been offering to define any thought that is *behind* the novel-long tale. The tale itself *is* the thought; my clumsy commentary is meant as an aid to perceiving that the delicate perfection of Lawrence's art-speech can be duly appreciated only as the precision and completeness of the thinking.

—F. R. Leavis, "The Captain's Doll," *Thought, Words, and Creativity: Art and Thought in Lawrence* (New York: Oxford University Press, 1976): pp. 94–95, 116–121.

FREDERICK P. W. MCDOWELL ON THE CAPTAIN'S CHARACTER

[Frederick P. W. McDowell is Emeritus Professor of English at the University of Iowa. He has published books on E. M. Forster and Ellen Glasgow, and has written on Shaw, Lawrence, Hardy, Auden, Conrad, and Angus Wilson. In this extract he discusses the Captain's mythic journey.]

There is something extraordinary about the Captain, a preternatural or supernatural aspect, a suggestion that outside powers centered in the heavenly bodies operate through him, a hint of the demonic (as Widmer maintains) that gives him reserves of authority and makes him indifferent at many times to the women in his life. At the beginning he overwhelms Hannele as he gazes on her "with his black eyes and that curious, bright, unseeing look that was more like second sight than direct human vision," as if he can divine truths denied to the faculties of ordinary mortals. He manifests a ruggedness of spirit, an objectivity, and a contempt for mundane trivialities when he turns "as if he heard something in the stars," and when he speaks in a "slow, musical voice, with its sing-song note of hopeless indifference." It is as if he heard the music of the spheres and as if for him "all the morning stars sang together." His air of mystery piques Hannele, and he seems to her "as if one of the men from Mars were loving her." She loses all volition as she falls under his hypnotic spell: "And she was heavy and spell-bound, and she loved the spell that bound her. But also she didn't love it." He has her fundamental being in his grasp, making her, as it were, a psychic prisoner of a phantom or demon lover: he is to her "as unreal as a person in a dream, whom one has never heard of in actual life." When he comes back to her in the Austrian Alps, she again reacts to his mystery and to a remoteness in him, at once formidable and fascinating, as she sees him "standing a long way off from her, beyond some border-line," seemingly an other-worldly visitant or a cherished phantom in human form. Sometimes his influence is Satanic as she identifies him and her passion for him with the serpent, in Lawrence's view "the symbol of the fluid, rapid, startling movement of life within us" that can be "half-divine, half-demonish." "She could feel the snake biting her heart" when her desire mounts and she succumbs in thought to his charm.

Yet at times she detects in her lover less than a full commitment to her, and she dramatizes her inchoate reservations about him by making the doll. This doll is a work of art, Hannele having obtained a local reputation for her craft and having earned her living by it. The Captain initially congratulates her, saying that she has really "got" him, thinking to himself that it "was an extraordinary likeness of himself, true even to the smooth parting of his hair and his peculiar way of fixing his dark eyes." He ultimately feels dissatisfied with this image precisely because Hannele has not really "got" him in his depths. She senses, with justification, however, that her lover is in part a doll, "a barren . . . dead puppet," since he is unwilling at this point to express in the domain of personal relationships his capacious inner powers. Her resentment translates outward into her actions as she fashions the doll, working with pins, treating it roughly, and sexually demeaning her lover by fashioning tartan trews to cover in the effigy the legs about which she had developed a fetishlike fixation.

Despite the richness of his elemental being, the Captain has become, with respect to his wife, the slave of convention; his wife has made an automaton of him. Hannele senses the falsity of her lover's existence with his wife after the latter comes to "rescue" him from an entanglement with a German woman. In a well-known comic sequence Mrs. Hepburn mistakes the identity of the mistress after her polite boast to Hannele that "we Irish all have a touch of second sight, I believe." Mrs. Hepburn is sure that her rival is Mitchka, Hannele's friend and roommate; Mrs. Hepburn's complacency, vulgarity, manipulativeness, and hypocrisy appall Hannele. She is even more aghast when Mrs. Hepburn reveals that her husband has sworn to her on bended knee that he would devote his life to making her happy.

Later in the tale the Captain admits that his wife had in fact made a doll of him and so confirms Hannele's intuitions that had led her also to make a doll of him. His acquiescence in a joyless lovemaking with his wife alienates Hannele. He has been false, she feels, to his better nature; in her view he should either have renewed the marital relationship with enthusiasm or ended it. In acting out an empty ritual, he becomes a hypocrite and, as Widmer observes, "Eros as a natural desire for pleasuring someone else stands antithetical to all authentic passion and being." If Hannele had not caught in the doll all her lover's depths, she had nevertheless captured some of them as well as something of the mechanical quality of his present emotional life. After Mrs. Hepburn's revelations of the "adoration-lust" that Alexander had displayed toward her, Hannele is radically disillusioned with him. Despite her overpowering disenchantment, she had enough perspective to realize that the illusion of passional fulfillment which she has experienced with him relates to the true depths of his being. If this satisfaction has been an illusion, yet it is, she thinks, more genuine than her revulsion at this moment. The spell with which he charmed her still holds her though she has become restive after she sees him with his wife: "And the strange gargoyle smile, fixed, when he caressed her with his hand under the chin! Life is all a choice. And if she chose the glamour, the magic, the charm, the illusion, the spell!" She faces a dilemma, for her instincts draw her to the Captain even when her intelligence sees him disparagingly as the husband "of that little lady." When his wife fortuitously falls out a hotel window and dies, the Captain finds himself emotionally drained, and he can no longer respond to the sensual depths in his mistress that had previously entranced him. ⟨. . .⟩

At his core Captain Alexander Hepburn is life-enkindling despite his entrapment in a meaningless marriage. The darkness that Hannele finds enveloping him cloaks a fierce light within, a darkness that gives him the power to venture into the unknown. The genuine instincts of his psyche lead him to a life-enhancing woman, Hannele, though at first he had refused to regard her with full seriousness. Mrs. Hepburn is not the only psychic prisoner in the marriage; her husband is also one until her sudden death frees him. The "adoration-lust" with which he had enshrined her continues to exert its influence over him; her death but accentuates the apathy he had felt in her presence. He rejects, however, the titillations offered by the nubile women who would adore him as a mate, just as he had adored his wife; and he reasserts his basic self, acting in the same spirit as Lawrence did in *Studies in Classic American Literature*, when he distinguished his own vital identity from the conformism implicit in Benjamin Franklin's attitude:

> "That I am I."
> "That my soul is a dark forest."
> "That my known self will never be more than a little clearing in the forest."
> "That gods, strange gods, come forth from the forest into the clearing of my known self, and then go back."
> "That I must have the courage to let them come and go."
> "That I will never let mankind put anything over me, but that I will try always to recognize and submit to the gods in me and the gods in other men and women."

The Captain, like Lawrence himself, assumes a vatic stance when he bursts beyond the artifices of his society and in his own way illustrates the motivations that Lawrence ascribed to the Europeans in coming to America: "To slough the old European consciousness completely" and then "To grow a new skin underneath, a new form." Hepburn, like Hannele, attains a reordered psyche; they both also participate in a mythic journey as Lawrence formulates it: "True myth concerns itself centrally with the onward adventure of the integral soul." The modern individual, discouraged by lifeless tradition and materialism, often lacks the courage "to withdraw at last into his own soul's stillness and aloneness, and *then*, passionately and faithfully, to strive for the living future." Once he attains such mastery and such vision, Hepburn senses still an incompleteness, and so he attempts to encompass the secondary law of all organic life as Lawrence articulates it in *Studies in Classic American Literature*: "each organism only lives through contact with other matter, assimilation, and contact with other life."

Realizing that "man doth not live by bread alone" and that "he lives even more essentially from the nourishing creative flow between himself and another or others," Hepburn finds, after his wife dies and he leaves the army, that memories of Hannele flood his being. He cannot now deny his demonic creativity, and with a flash of intuition he perceives that his future must lie with the most vital woman he has known. A proud isolation and a demonic intensity are not incompatible, the Captain discovers, with dynamic commitment to another human being. He now admits that "conscience is the being's consciousness, when the individual is conscious *in toto*, when he knows in full. . . . Every man must live as far as he can by his own soul's conscience."

—Frederick P. W. McDowell, "'The Individual in His Pure Singleness': Theme and Symbol in *The Captain's Doll*," in *The Challenge of D. H. Lawrence*, edited by Michael Squires and Keith Cushman (Madison: University of Wisconsin Press, 1990): pp. 144–46, 148–49.

Plot Summary of
St. Mawr

The first version of *St. Mawr*, a novel-length work, was finished during the first half of June 1924, and it was rewritten by July 7 of the same year. It was first published in London together with the story "The Princess" in May 1925; later, in June 1925, Knopf in America published it as a separate publication.

The writing of D. H. Lawrence often demonstrates his uncanny gift of appearing to know what it is like to be an animal; he almost seems to be able to enter the souls of animals. The finest display of this gift is *St. Mawr*.

The narrative of the tale moves swiftly: it proceeds from London, where the novel opens, to Westminster, then shifts to Shropshire; we follow the main characters' horse ride on their way to Oxfordshire. Before the story's closure, there is a major shift of setting to America. This final phase is set in New Mexico at the Las Chivas ranch in the Rocky Mountains. (This was based on the Lawrences' Lobo Ranch— later renamed Kiowa Ranch—at Questa, 17 miles from Taos, where the novel was written and where the Lawrences lived between May and October 1924 and between April and September 1925).

The characters in the story are sharply and brilliantly drawn. Lou Witt, an American woman of 24, is eventually married to Rico Carrington, an Australian baronet's son, with whom she had a bohemian affair while they were both in Rome. They settle in Westminster, where Rico pursues a fashionable career as a portrait painter in the high circles of society in London and becomes quite successful. The reader senses that Lou, meanwhile, is an outsider, "like a gypsy who is at home anywhere and nowhere: all this made up her charm and her failure. She didn't quite belong."

From almost the very beginning, we are told that Rico and Lou are bound to each other by a "nervous attachment" rather than by sexual love or spontaneous passion. Note Lawrence's psychological insight:

> Each was curiously under the domination of the other. They were pair—they had to be together. Yet quite soon they shrank from one another. This attachment of the will and the nerves was destructive.

> As soon as one felt strong, the other felt ill. As soon as the ill one recovered strength, down went the one who had been well.

Soon, the marriage became more like a platonic friendship, marriage without sex.

> Sex was shattering and exhausting, they shrank from it, and became like brother and sister. And the lack of physical relation was a secret source of uneasiness and chagrin to both of them.

Lou fully recognizes Rico's powerlessness as a man only when she is showed the magnificent but temperamental stallion, St. Mawr. She is captivated by the horse, and experiences a kind of epiphany in which an "ancient understanding" floods into her soul. She comes to a complete realization that she must abandon her commonplace self in order to seek the reality of deeper self and realms of otherness. She buys St. Mawr for Rico and at the same time acquires Lewis, a mystical Welshman who attends and understands the horse.

Mrs. Witt, Lou's mother, along with her Mexican-Indian servant, Phoenix, takes a house in Shropshire that overlooks a churchyard. (The reader learns later that this gives her the opportunity to watch funerals, something she enjoys.) Lou and Rico attend a dinner party held by Mrs. Witt, and there a lively discussion is sparked on the Great God Pan. Lawrence unmistakably speaks through this conversation:

> "Pan was the hidden mystery—the hidden cause. That's how it was a Great God. Pan wasn't *he* at all: not even a Great God. He was Pan. All: what you see when you see in full. In the daytime you see the thing. But if your third eye is open, which sees only the things that can't be seen, you may see Pan within the thing, hidden: you may see with your third eye, which is darkness."

In due course the topic will be continued privately by Mrs. Witt and Lou when they come to the conclusion that there is no true "Pan-Quality" in today's world. (By "Pan-Quality," Lawrence means a wild life that burns straight from the source.)

The central event takes place when St. Mawr, frightened by a dead snake, suddenly "explodes." Rico tries to restrain him, but the horse rears, and Rico falls, breaking his ribs and crushing his ankle.

Riding back home, Lou has a vision of evil. Here Lawrence leaves the narrative and embarks on one of his well-known prophetic passages (for almost six pages), without breaking the story's rhythm.

She became aware of evil, evil, evil, rolling in great waves over the earth. Always she had thought there was no such thing—only a mere negation of good. Now, like an ocean to whose surface she had risen, she saw the dark-grey waves of evil rearing in a great tide.

And it had swept mankind away without mankind's knowing. It had caught up the nations as the rising ocean might lift the fishes, and was sweeping them on a great tide of evil. They did not know. The people did not know. They did not even wish it. They wanted to be good and to have everything joyful and enjoyable. Everything joyful and enjoyable: for everybody. This was what they wanted; if you asked them.

Lawrence's technique makes use of repetition. Anthony Burgess puts it this way: "Having found certain *mots justes*, . . . he is not content to let the single sounding reverberate. There is a liturgical quality about the restatement." This point is illustrated in many passages.

Eventually, both mother and daughter fall even more deeply in love with St. Mawr. When the stallion's vitality is threatened (with Rico's approval, the horse is to be gelded), Mrs. Witt rides with Lewis and St. Mawr to Oxfordshire, where she arranges for all of them (Lou, Lewis, Phoenix, St. Mawr, and herself) to go to America. While riding through the countryside, she proposes to Lewis, who rejects her. Meanwhile, Lou loses patience with the superficiality and hollowness of life around her. She goes to London to make final arrangements for her departure to America. Lawrence's voice is persuasive in these passages that show his own profound revulsion with polite tea-table conversation.

The last chapter proceeds at a restrained tempo as the reader encounters Lou's last refuge—an abandoned, goat-ruined ranch high in the Rocky Mountains. Lou buys Las Chivas (meaning she-goats) despite foreboding signs. Lawrence's again demonstrates his marvelous awareness of nature in his poetic account of the ranch's history.

The golden stallion St. Mawr is Lawrence's symbol for the soul's struggle for independent self-hood. As the story closes, the reader, however, is not certain if Lou will actually find in the wilderness of the Rocky Mountains the Great God Pan or his deep "blood-consciousness." ❀

List of Characters in
St. Mawr

Lou Witt (Lady Carrington) is an American from a moderately rich Louisiana family. She is very sophisticated. At 25 she marries Sir Henry Carrington (Rico), but soon enough she begins to fully comprehend his "powerlessness." When the stallion's masculinity is threatened, she flees to America, sick of the company of people, and buys a ranch where she can freely give herself to other, unseen presences.

Rico (Sir Henry Carrington) is an Australian artist, the son of a government official in Melbourne, who has been made a baronet. He dutifully marries Lou Witt and they settle in England where he becomes a trendy portrait painter. Rico is injured in an accident with St. Mawr and becomes filled with bitter feelings toward the stallion. By the end of the novel, Rico welcomes the flirtation of Flora Manby.

Mrs. Rachael Witt is the mother of Lou. She shares her daughter's admiration for the stallion. When she becomes exhausted by society, she flees to America with the horse, her daughter, Lewis, and Phoenix. In Lewis she sees of the world "beyond," but he rejects her proposal. In America she falls into a state of apathy, passiveness, and indifference.

Morgan Lewis is St. Mawr's groom; he is a dark, mystical Welshman who understands the horse and speaks to him in Welsh. When Mrs. Witt offers herself in marriage to him, he proudly refuses: "No woman shall touch my body, and mock and despise me. No Woman."

Phoenix (Gerónimo Trujilo) is Mrs. Witt's servant, an American of mixed Spanish and Indian blood. On returning to America, he is prepared to sell himself to a woman in exchange for the excitements of the modern world.

Flora Manby is a gaudy and cheerful girl who is glad she lives in the 1920s. She blatantly flirts with Rico. Rico stays overnight at her house on one occasion, and the narrator insinuates that from the very beginning there is more between them than mere flirtation.

St. Mawr is a beautiful stallion with a "sharp questioning glint" in his big, black eyes. He represents the spirit of life itself. ❀

Critical Views on
St. Mawr

F. R. LEAVIS ON *ST. MAWR* AS LAWRENCE'S
DRAMATIC POEM

[F. R. Leavis (1895–1978) was founder of the review
Scrutiny, Fellow and Director of English Studies at
Downing College, Cambridge, and University Reader in
English. He achieved worldwide fame in his lifetime as
teacher, critic, lecturer, and writer. Among his publications
are *New Bearings in English Poetry* (1932), *Revaluation*
(1936), *The Great Tradition* (1948), *Anna Karenina and
Other Essays* (1967), *Dickens the Novelist* (1970; with his
wife Q. D. Leavis), and *The Critic as Anti-Philosopher*
(1982). In this extract taken from his book *D. H. Lawrence:
Novelist*, he asserts that *St. Mawr* presents "a creative and
technical originality more remarkable than that of *The
Waste Land*."]

St. Mawr, I suppose, would commonly be described as a long short-
story—a *nouvelle*, rather than a novel. Actually, that description, with
its limiting effect, has a marked infelicity. It certainly doesn't suggest
the nature or weight of the astonishing work of genius that
Lawrence's 'dramatic poem' is. *St. Mawr* seems to me to present a
creative and technical originality more remarkable than that of *The
Waste Land*, being, as that poem is not, completely achieved, a full
and self-sufficient creation. It can hardly strike the admirer as
anything but major.

The comparative reference isn't random: *St. Mawr*, too, has the
Waste Land for theme. To say this is to suggest scope as well as
intensity, and the suggestion isn't idle. There are, besides the horse
and the two grooms, only three main actors, but, at the end of the
hundred and eighty-odd pages, it is as if we had had a representative
view of the civilized world. Lawrence's art, then, commands a
pregnancy and a concentrated force not suggested by 'tale' or
'*nouvelle*.' Yet what strikes us in the opening of *St. Mawr* is not a
portentousness or any kind of tension, but a freedom—something
extraordinarily like careless ease:

Lou Witt had had her own way so long, that by the age of twenty-five she didn't know where she was. Having one's own way landed one completely at sea.

To be sure for a while she had failed in her grand love affair with Rico. And then she had had something really to despair about. But even that had worked out as she wanted. Rico had come back to her, and was dutifully married to her. And now, when she was twenty-five and he was three months older, they were a charming married couple. He flirted with other women still, to be sure. He wouldn't be the handsome Rico if he didn't. But she had 'got' him. Oh yes! You had only to see the uneasy backward glance at her, from his big blue eyes: just like a horse that is edging away from its master: to know how completely he was mastered.

She, with her odd little *museau*, not exactly pretty, but very attractive; and her quaint air of playing at being well-bred, in a sort of charade game; and her queer familiarity with foreign cities and foreign languages; and the lurking sense of being an outsider everywhere, like a sort of gipsy, who is at home anywhere and nowhere: all this made up her charm and her failure. She didn't quite belong.

Of course she was American: Louisiana family, moved down to Texas. And she was moderately rich, with no close relation except her mother. But she had been sent to school in France when she was twelve, and since she had finished school, she had drifted from Paris to Palermo, Biarritz to Vienna and back via Munich to London, then down again to Rome. Only fleeting trips to her America.

So what sort of American was she, after all?

And what sort of European was she either? She didn't 'belong' anywhere. Perhaps most of all in Rome, among the artists and the Embassy people.

It was in Rome she had met Rico. He was an Australian, son of a government official in Melbourne, who had been made a baronet. So one day Rico would be Sir Henry, as he was the only son. Meanwhile, he floated round Europe on a very small allowance—his father wasn't rich in capital—and was being an artist.

The economy of those opening pages, establishing the present from which the drama starts, is very remarkable. For what looks like carelessness—the relaxed, idiomatic and even slangy familiarity—is actually precision and vivid firsthandness. And we soon discover that there is no limit to the power of easy and inevitable transitions. For Lawrence writes out of the full living language with a flexibility and a creative freedom for which I can think of no parallel in modern times. His writing seems to have the careless ease of extraordinarily fluent and racy speech; but you see, if you stop to cast a critical eye back over the page, that everything is precisely and easily *right*—the slangy colloquialism, the flippant cliché given an emotional intensity, the 'placing' sardonic touch, and, when it comes (as it so marvellously can at any moment), the free play of poetic imagery and imaginative evocation, sensuous and focally suggestive.

The opening pages are sardonic comedy, and it looks as if we are going to have merely a variant of that admirable short story, *Mother and Daughter*. Rico and Lou, though 'they reacted badly on each other's nerves,' and he 'couldn't stand Mrs. Witt, and Mrs. Witt couldn't stand him.' ⟨. . .⟩

The marriage is not a success—as Mrs. Witt, 'watching as it were from outside the fence, like a potent well-dressed demon, full of uncanny energy and a shattering sort of sense,' realizes almost immediately. And we note with what easy economy the different values of the main actors in the drama are established: Rico, representative of modern civilized 'life'; the formidable Mrs. Witt, the American female, insatiably dominating, who hardly disguises her contempt for him; and Lou, who can't happily accept either what Rico *is* or her mother's satisfaction in mere destructive negativity. Lou's sense of the nature of the failure of her marriage is brought to full consciousness by the stallion, St. Mawr, and we may note how we are sensitized beforehand to take his significance as soon as he makes his entrance. An instance occurred in the opening passage quoted above: 'You had only to see the uneasy backward glance at her, from his big blue eyes: just like a horse that is edging away from its master: to know how completely he was mastered.' And here is the consequence of Mrs. Witt's will to ride in the Park, where Lou, 'for very decency's sake' ('Mrs. Witt was *so* like a smooth, levelled, gun-metal pistol, Lou had to be a sort of sheath'), must ride with her:

> 'Rico dear, you must get a horse.'
> The tone was soft and southern and drawling, but the overtone had a decisive finality. In vain Rico squirmed—he had a way of writhing and squirming which perhaps he had caught at Oxford. In vain he protested that he couldn't ride, and that he didn't care for riding. He got quite angry, and his handsome arched nose tilted and his upper lip lifted from his teeth, like a dog that is going to bite. Yet daren't quite bite.
> And that was Rico. He daren't quite bite. Not that he was really afraid of the others. He was afraid of himself, once he let himself go. He might rip up in an eruption of life-long anger all this pretty-pretty

picture of a charming young wife and a delightful little home and a
fascinating success as a painter of fashionable, and at the same time
'great' portraits: with colour, wonderful colour, and at the same time
form, marvellous form. He had composed this little *tableau vivant*
with great effort. He didn't want to erupt like some suddenly wicked
horse—Rico was really more like a horse than a dog, a horse that
might go nasty any moment. For the time, he was good, very good,
dangerously good.

Rico is the antithesis of St. Mawr; he represents the irremediable
defeat of all that St. Mawr stands for. Nevertheless, as the passage
just quoted conveys, the frustrated drives of life are still there, down
below, always threatening trouble in Rico and making security and
satisfaction impossible. He's always in danger of 'making a break' of
the kind for which St. Mawr becomes notorious. ⟨. . .⟩

To call St. Mawr a poetic symbol doesn't help much. To call him a
sexual symbol is positively misleading. In fact, this 'story about a
stallion' refutes in the most irrefutable of ways, for those who take
what it offers, the common notion that Lawrence is obsessed with
sex, or preaches some religion of sex, or is more preoccupied with
sex than the T. S. Eliot of *The Waste Land*. The marriage between
Lou and Rico, this attachment of the will and the nerves, does
indeed, the datum is given us, fail at the level of sex, in becoming
'more like a friendship, Platonic'; but the failure there is the index of
a failure far transcending that.

St. Mawr seemed to look at Lou 'out of another world': this kind
of suggestion in Lawrence, irresistibly (one would have thought) as
his art conveys it, is often dismissed as 'romantic'—that is, as an
indulgence of imagination or fancy that cannot, by the mature, be
credited with any real significance or taken seriously. The reader
who is inclined to 'place' so the rendering, quoted from above, of
the first effect of St. Mawr on Lou should pay heed to what
follows—to the account of the immediate consequence for Lou's
relations with Rico. 'No matter where she was, what she was doing,
at the back of her consciousness loomed a great, over-aweing figure
out of a dark background.'

—F. R. Leavis, *D. H. Lawrence: Novelist* (New York: Simon and
Schuster, 1955): pp. 225–26, 227–28, 229.

RICHARD POIRIER ON LOU WITT'S ATTEMPT TO FIND
RENEWAL IN THE WILDERNESS

[Richard Poirier is one of the leading American literary critics. He is the author of *Comic Sense of Henry James: A Study of the Early Novels* (1967), *Norman Mailer* (1972), *Robert Frost: The Work of Knowing* (1977), *Renewal of Literature: Emersonian Reflection* (1987), *Poetry and Pragmatism* (1992), and most recently *Trying It Out in America: Literary and Other Performances* (1998). In this extract, taken from his book *A World Elsewhere*, he emphasizes Lawrence's modulation in the story.]

Lawrence's immersion in American literature is everywhere evident in the story. The heroine, Lou Witt, living in England with her mother and married to an Australian named Rico, chooses, like many American heroes and heroines before her, to disassociate herself from a polite society and from a marriage, both parodied in the opening pages, and to find renewal in the wilderness. She retreats to the New Mexican desert, there to find a spirit "that wants her." The geographical movement of the story has obvious historical and literary precedents: from old to new worlds, from England (the "close, hedged-and-fenced English landscape. Everything enclosed, enclosed to stifling") to Mexico (where "The great circling landscape lived its own life"), from a land without the opportunities proffered by unfilled space ("Not a space, not a speck of this country that wasn't humanized, occupied by the human claim") to a landscape for which "man did not exist." But before this geographical evocation of two worlds, Lou has already contrived them in her imagination and has done so in a manner which, again, suggests a classic feature of American literature: when she first sees St. Mawr, an equestrian Moby-Dick, a domesticated Big Ben, the horse "seemed to look at her out of another world." While imagining this "other" world, she can, like Thoreau, or Faulkner's heroes, or Hemingway in his sporting or hunting stories, or Melville's Ahab, think of those around her in hierarchies that appeal not to social institutions but rather to the mysterious powers potent but thwarted in animal life. Lewis, the groom, thereby becomes elevated above her husband Rico, by "the aristocracy of invisible powers, the greater influences, nothing to do with human society."

Lou's effort to promote the secret powers of St. Mawr within the context of English mannered society can only find a voice in the first half of the story that is largely destructive and satiric. The burden of this satiric effort is at first carried mostly by her mother, Mrs. Witt. Her ironies are full of a self-loathing which Lou recognizes as a doomed alternative to the deadening social chic of her husband. But once St. Mawr has revealed himself in Texas as no more than a fawning stud, Lou finds in the landscape of New Mexico, in something no human being has tamed, a further call not merely to criticism of human society but to potencies beyond it. She tries to imagine for herself some creative alternative both to society and to the ironic-satiric treatment of it in which she had joined Mrs. Witt while both were entrapped within the terms and vocabularies of a social set. In a sense *St. Mawr* includes within itself the two attitudes toward existent environments which I've located in American literature: the one imitative, often satiric, often critical, but essentially submissive, in being merely corrective, to the necessary reality of established society; the other creative, daring, often ridiculous in the effort to express a creative ideal of alternative environment where the self can unite its powers with presumably harmonious natural forces.

Where Lawrence is most English in the story is in the degree to which even at the end he finds it necessary to be skeptical of the possibilities Lou is affirming. The skepticism expresses itself most noticeably in his never consorting fully with her tendencies as a symbolist: he himself never confirms the importance she assigns to St. Mawr or to the New Mexican landscape. Whatever support her symbolisms receive from his writing or from his narrative voice is in the marvelous beauty of his descriptions. If she is a symbolist, he more accurately displays what Gertrude Stein meant by remarking that "Description is explanation": the power and magnificence of landscape and of animal life is precisely, so Lawrence implies, that it is *not* available as metaphor. Lawrence's place in the book is a clarified version of Melville's in *Moby-Dick* when it comes to his subscribing to the symbolist tendencies of the central character. Skepticism of this kind, however, need not and does not modify the grandeurs of description in which Melville and Lawrence like to indulge. The admiration of the writers in both cases goes not to the possible accuracy of a symbolist perspective but only to the heroic nobility of incentive behind it, its creative responsiveness to the things of this world.

In the tradition of American romantic literature, Lawrence values the redemptive power of imagination even when its particular exertions are preposterous. The effort, the struggle to change the world, to alter even the laws of nature here, as in Emerson and in all of James, brings rewards only to the imagination and to the consciousness of participants and witnesses, rewards without any practical benefit or visible objectification. The struggle may be with the alien forces in nature that Emerson did not feel it necessary to acknowledge so fully as did Melville, but it is also with those inheritances of old thinking, of old formulas, and of language itself which Emerson continually laments, with no illusions that it is ever possible fully to escape from them.

—Richard Poirier, *A World Elsewhere: The Place of Style in American Literature* (New York: Oxford University Press, 1966): pp. 41–44.

KEITH SAGAR ON *ST. MAWR* AND THE FULLNESS OF BEING

[Keith Sagar is Reader in English Literature at the University of Manchester. His publications include *Life of D. H. Lawrence* (1989), *D. H. Lawrence: Life into Art* (1985), *Achievement of Ted Hughes* (1983, editor), and *Challenge of Ted Hughes* (1994, editor). In this extract, taken from his book *The Art of D. H. Lawrence* (1966), he reflects on Lawrence's representation of St. Mawr as symbolic of reality's living unity.]

The prose of *St. Mawr* is more flexible than any Lawrence had written since the war. It moves subtly from an apparent flippancy in the description of Rico and his relationship with Lou ('a charming married couple') to an earnestness and stature appropriate to the new dimension which St. Mawr brings into the novel and into Lou's life. The two styles meet and deliberately clash in such passages as this:

She could not bear the triviality and superficiality of her human relationships. Looming like some god out of the darkness was the head of that horse, with the wide, terrible, questioning eyes. And she felt that it forbade her to be her ordinary, commonplace self. It forbade her to be just Rico's wife, young Lady Carrington, and all that.

Her life with Rico has been purely attitude. She had not known that relationships could be based on anything other than attitude. The prose associated with St. Mawr is, like him, the opposite of attitude and triviality. The light, sardonic touch of the opening is appropriate only to the world of attitudes:

> But now she realised that, with men and women, everything is an attitude only when something else is lacking. Something is lacking and they are thrown back on their own devices. That black fiery flow in the eyes of the horse was not 'attitude.' It was something much more terrifying, and real, the only thing that was real. Gushing from the darkness in menace and question, and blazing out in the splendid body of the horse.

The question St. Mawr asks Lou is 'Are you alive?'. He testifies to a mode, a dimension of living which is unquestionably real, if dangerous, and challenges her to enter it. To Rico, St. Mawr is merely another pose:

> 'He'd be marvellous in a Composition. That colour.'

The choice she is offered is 'between two worlds.' She must 'meet him half-way':

> But half-way across from our human world to that terrific equine twilight was not a small step. It was a step, she knew, that Rico could never take. She knew it. But she was prepared to sacrifice Rico.

The other world is again associated with the world from which the snake was a messenger:

> She realised that St. Mawr drew his hot breaths in another world from Rico's, from our world. Perhaps the old Greek horses had lived in St. Mawr's world. And the old Greek heroes, even Hippolytus, had known it.
>
> With their strangely naked equine heads, and something of a snake in their way of looking around, and lifting their sensitive, dangerous muzzles, they moved in a prehistoric twilight where all things loomed phantasmagoric, all on one plane, sudden presences suddenly jutting out of the matrix. It was another world, an older, heavily potent world. And in this world the horse was swift and fierce and supreme, undominated and unsurpassed. ⟨. . .⟩

The first clause of the law of life which Lawrence formulates in *Reflections on the Death of a Porcupine* is this:

> Any creature that attains to its own fullness of being, its own *living* self, becomes unique, a nonpareil. It has its place in the fourth dimension, the heaven of existence, and there it is perfect, it is beyond comparison.

So little fullness of being has Lou at the beginning of *St. Mawr* that she is almost unsure of her own reality or that of the people she knew—'entirely contained within their cardboard let's-be-happy world':

> The talk, the eating and drinking, the flirtation, the endless dancing: it all seemed far more bodiless and in a strange way, wraith-like, than any fairy story. She seemed to be eating Barmecide food, that had been conjured up out of thin air, by the power of words. She seemed to be talking to handsome, young, bare-faced unrealities, not men at all: as she slid about with them, in the perpetual dance, they too seemed to have been conjured up out of air, merely for this soaring, slithering dance business. And she should not believe that, when the lights went out, they wouldn't melt back into thin air again and complete nonentity.

Against all this 'seeming' is a new vision, whose authenticity St. Mawr attests, produces, indeed, by his catalytic presence.

Coleridge said of the symbol that it 'always partakes of the reality which it renders intelligible, and while it enunciates the whole, abides itself as a living part in that unity of which it is the living representative.' The unity of which St. Mawr is the living representative, the matrix out of which he looms, is the divine circuit in which all living things are charged with God, or with the gods, as Lawrence at this stage phrases it.

St. Mawr, like a Hopkins creature, is charged with God, his body glowing red with power, 'looming like a bonfire in the dark.' To Lou he is a visitation, he rings and tells of God:

> When he reared his head and neighed from his deep chest, like deep wind-bells resounding, she seemed to hear the echoes of another darker, more spacious, more dangerous, more splendid world than ours, that was beyond her.

When Lawrence names his god in *St. Mawr* it is Pan—'the god that is hidden in everything . . . the hidden mystery, the hidden cause

... what you see when you see in full.' In a letter to Willard Johnson, editor of *The Laughing Horse*, from London on 9 January 1924, Lawrence developed the identification of the horse with Pan:

> And over here the Horse is dead: he'll kick his heels no more. I don't know whether it's the pale Galilean who has triumphed, or a paleness paler than the pallor even of Jesus ... When Jesus was born, the spirits wailed round the Mediterranean: Pan is dead. Great Pan is dead ... It would be a terrible thing if the horse in us died for ever, as he seems to have died in Europe.

Pan is also, as the snake was, identified with the Christian devil:

> The old god Pan became the Christian devil, with the cloven hoofs and the horns, the tail, and the laugh of derision. Old Nick, the Old Gentleman who is responsible for all our wickednesses, but especially our sensual excesses—this is all that is left of the Great God Pan.

St. Mawr is part of Lawrence's campaign to reinstate Pan-Lucifer in his original potency and brightness. In the letter to Johnson he goes on to gloss the symbol of the centaur. It stands, first, for Horse-sense:

> And then, a laugh, a loud, sensible Horse Laugh. After that, these same passions, glossy and dangerous in the flanks. And after these again, hoofs, irresistible, slintering hoofs, that can kick the walls of the world down.

'Wouldn't a man be wonderful in whom Pan hadn't fallen!' cries Mrs. Witt, her hard-boiled, sardonic exterior beginning to break up under St. Mawr's influence. 'Did you ever see Pan in the man you loved?' she asks Lou.

> 'As I see Pan in St. Mawr?—no mother!' Her lips began to tremble and the tears came to her eyes.

—Keith Sagar, *The Art of D. H. Lawrence* (Cambridge, U.K.: Cambridge University Press, 1966): pp. 151–54.

FRANK KERMODE ON THE DOUBLING OF NARRATIVE AND SYMBOLIC SENSE

[Sir Frank Kermode is Professor of English at Cambridge University. Among his best known books are *Romantic Image, The Classic, The Sense of an Ending, Continuities, Shakespeare, Spencer and Donne: Renaissance Essays, The Uses of Error* and *The Genesis of Secrecy*. In this excerpt he states that the conclusion of *St. Mawr* is one of Lawrence's most fully imagined pieces.]

St. Mawr is a focus of contention; it can be a leading document in the case against Lawrence as well as for him. It strikes me as one of the most achieved of his works. A woman's rejection of what passes for sex in the modern world, her acceptance of separateness and authentic contact with the cosmos—stated thus the theme sounds almost too familiar. But the book says much more. I think of it as the work which best shows how the insights of the Hawthorne essay were reflected in Lawrence's own writing.

The horse St. Mawr has ancestors, notably in the dream described in *Fantasia*, in *The Boy in the Bush*, and in the apocalyptic animals of *The Rainbow*. Yet the figuration is new. Lou's marriage to Rico, the disoriented American woman to the Anglo-Australian hollow man, is also of a familiar type, the exhaustingly nervous, frictional, peaceless union. What distinguishes it is the density with which Rico's half-life as man and artist and friend is rendered; and his relationship with St. Mawr, which is one of hatred between primitive male blood-knowledge and the highly strung parody of maleness that the man represents. The narrative shows how the different, brutal life of the horse—so insistently representative of 'another world,' the non-human world of Pan—damages Rico and changes Lou's world to one of separateness in an inhuman landscape.

Most impressive is the doubling of narrative and symbolic senses. The grooms Phoenix and Lewis, Indian and Celt, are skillfully characterised but also bear heavy doctrinal charges. Even in the difficult scene when Lewis speaks of his beliefs, and argues with Lou's mother, Mrs. Witt, about the meaning of the shooting star, one is not inclined to speak of self-indulgence, though the passage certainly relates to a new strain of apocalypticism that now obsesses Lawrence. Mrs. Witt herself is presented in real depth—a demonstration of defensive worldly intelligence, a middle-aged woman defending herself with candour, irony and death-worship, against a world grown intolerably trivial. She has a doctrinal role, but it does not usurp personality. So with the New Mexican landscape of the conclusion; its metaphysical implications do not reduce its physical presence. It is the antithesis of England's countryside, which has grown 'little, old, unreal'—the American wilderness into which Lawrence, following so many admired New World authors, sends his heroine to find herself. The Pan whom they had merely discussed in Shropshire confronts them alive in New Mexico, as Lawrence observed in the essay 'Pan in America.'

The sense of complex and hopeless corruption, out of which the doctrine is born, here takes precedence over the doctrine. Not that the book lacks doctrine. There is the usual racism; there are discussions of favourite themes—the overvaluation of intellect, the need to go beyond love, and 'evil, evil, evil, rolling in great waves over the earth . . . a soft, subtle thing, soft as water . . . a rapid return to the chaos.' Even St. Mawr is part of this evil, though Rico is the worst part. It is the evil which will give fascism its chance. In this way the preaching and the narrative conspire with a kind of urgency to speak of the same thing. Everybody is part of the evil: Mrs Witt cutting Lewis's hair and, even while she loves him, unable to respect his separateness; the ultimate parasitic cheapness of Phoenix; the evil eye and rearing legs of St. Mawr, tainted by the 'vulgar evil' of men. Lou attributes to the stallion a despair at the ignobility of men which accounts for his abstention from the mares. But he recovers his sex in New Mexico, which is for her a place of therapeutic chastity and solitude.

Why does the woman need to renounce sex? In Shropshire the wife of the Dean, attributing the violence of St. Mawr to 'evil male cruelty,' is making what for Lawrence was a characteristic mistake of degenerate womanhood and decadent Christianity: with a fine touch he compares the 'mean cruelty' of her humanitarianism with Rico's 'eunuch cruelty.' It is from all this that Lou escapes. *Noli me tangere*; she goes beyond the touch of men into that otherness from which the truth alone comes. 'Man and woman should stay apart, till they have learned to be gentle with one another again.' She leaves the 'arctic horror' for the mountains of the south, alone—not as Birkin and Ursula left it, for Italy, together. She escapes from the 'friction,' leaving behind not only the rat-sexuality of Phoenix but even 'the illusion of the beautiful St. Mawr'; she embraces a positive chastity, knowing better than to expect the 'mystic new man.'

The conclusion of *St. Mawr* is one of Lawrence's most fully imagined pieces. The landscape is more splendid and awful than a man-god, a saviour; beautiful and brutal, it has horrors which are not those of civilisation and its 'Augean stables of metallic filth.' On a ranch subject to natural catastrophes—drought, packrats, disease— Lou passes beyond Law and Love, far beyond decadent sex sensation, choosing instead the wild America where 'a wild spirit wants me.' Her aspirations are questioned by her sceptical mother; but the mother is on the side of death, Lou on the more terrible side of life.

It is sometimes said that Lawrence got too much wrong: Rico's clothes, Lou's title, having St. Mawr ridden in Hyde Park, where stallions are forbidden, not seeing, as English horsemen would, that Rico's accident was his own fault, or that no lady would have behaved as Mrs. Witt did, startling the horse and endangering her son-in-law. Mr. Hough uses a good many such arguments to support his point: Lawrence, returning disgusted from the visit to England which provided the Shropshire scenes of the story, was guilty of a falseness in putting a pasteboard England in competition with a beautiful wild America; Lou is not really doing anything there anyway, and the problems of civilisation, though real enough, are not to be solved in this way. I do not feel the force of these difficulties, which seem at best trivial in the light of such a reading as that of Dr Leavis—surely the best study of any single Lawrence tale. *St. Mawr* avoids the diagrammatic quality that spoils *The Princess* (frigid white woman cruelly treated by sexually vengeful Indian) and the sensationalism of *None of That*, a story written a year or two later, in which a rich American woman is raped by six of the assistants of a Mexican Indian bullfighter. Such a story is evidence of Lawrence's desperate situation; a sense of horror and of a world ending may distort as well as quicken the narrative imagination. He was entering another bad time; in February 1925 he had his almost fatal illness, and in the following autumn he left New Mexico for good.

—Frank Kermode, *Lawrence* (Bungay, Suffolk: Fontana/Collins, 1973): pp. 111–14.

FREDERICK P. W. McDOWELL ON LOU WITT'S
STRUGGLE TOWARD 'INCREASED ILLUMINATION'

[Frederick P. W. McDowell is Emeritus Professor of English at the University of Iowa. He has published books on E. M. Forster and Ellen Glasgow, and has written on Shaw, Lawrence, Hardy, Auden, Conrad, and Angus Wilson. In this extract he describes *St. Mawr* as one of Lawrence's richest fictions that incessantly expands in the mind.]

St. Mawr has encouraged Lou to examine herself, to break through to a new awareness, and to struggle uncompromisingly toward 'increased illumination.' As a result of her vision of evil at the time of the accident to Rico, Lou is desperate as to how best to handle her situation, but decides that she at least can no longer be passive. Rather, she must struggle to achieve a sense of integrity as a human being, and, above all, she must struggle to prevent her new illumination from fading:

> The individual can but depart from the mass, and try to cleanse himself. Try to hold fast to the living thing, which destroys as it goes, but remains sweet. And, in his soul fight, fight, fight to preserve that which is life in him from the ghastly kisses and poison-bites of the myriad evil ones. Retreat to the desert, and fight. But in his soul adhere to that which is life itself, creatively destroying as it goes: destroying the stiff old thing to let the new bud come through. The one passionate principle of creative being, which recognises the natural good, and has a sword for the swarms of evil. Fights, fights, fights to protect itself. But with itself, is strong and at peace.

Lou's sentiments are analogous to those that Lawrence expressed in a contemporaneous letter, when he also emphasised the importance of strenuous effort: 'One fights and fights for that living something that stirs way down in the blood, and *creates* consciousness.'

From the first, St. Mawr had impressed Lou with the need to hold by her sense of the fitting and never to give way or to give in. On the ride to the Devil's Chair in Shropshire, overlooking the habitats of the ancient Celts, Lou identifies with 'the old fighting stock' that had once dwelt among the Welsh hills, and she decides that the people accompanying her on this ride are anaemic in comparison to these sensitive and imaginative peoples of long ago. In America Lou settles at her ranch, Las Chivas, as 'new blood to the attack' upon the subversive influences that surround it. Even to maintain intact her identity, she will learn that she will have to struggle against those very forces that also can promote a sense of well-being and renewal. She will have to commit herself to overcome the 'sordidness' of the primitive as such, in order to capture the 'inward vision' and the 'cleaner energy,' and to 'win from the crude wild nature the victory and the power to make another start.' Her renunciation of European 'civilisation' does not allow for passivity. Lou, accordingly, adopts the Lawrentian posture in America: 'As for the fight—subtly and eternally I fight, till something breaks in me.'

The courage that she finds so admirable in the ancient Celts and in St. Mawr is the quality which she emulates in New Mexico, again attesting to the surviving influence upon her there of St. Mawr. Courage is the attribute that is most electrifying in St. Mawr, the attribute most lacking in the decadent people surrounding Lou, and the attribute that she comes to value most as it enables her to forge a new philosophy. It is from St. Mawr that Lou derives the strength to recast her life and to cut herself off from the pleasures and the futilities of a polite society; as a life-serving force, he is not afraid to destroy if he must do so in order to create anew. St. Mawr gives her, in short, the power to resist the bogus and the determination to achieve a significant order of being by an active assertion of her powers, whatever the cost in immediate ease. In boldness, defiance, endurance, self-sufficiency and vigour, St. Mawr had seemed to her the only genuine embodiment of 'Pan,' the elemental life-principle, that she had encountered in England. When she reaches New Mexico, the landscape possesses a strange animistic energy as if its most significant aspect lies behind the outward phenomena that compose it. She finds 'Pan' in New Mexico, not in a human being but in the sublime landscape, though she is also awaiting a man who may truly embody the strength of that god. Lawrence had asserted in 'Pan in America' that in America 'we can still choose between the living universe of Pan, and the mechanical conquered universe of modern humanity.' In effect, Lou has made this choice, difficult as it has been for her to implement. In America, in short, she can catch a glimpse of the god Pan by opening her 'third eye,' her sharpened sensory powers which her English acquaintance Cartwright had described as indispensable for catching sight of this god. Pan, whom Lou had found in England in St. Mawr alone, has been transferred from him to inhere in the spreading New Mexican landscape, another instance of the stallion's presence with Lou in America. Like St. Mawr, Lou is now able to immerse herself in a world of primaeval nature. The New England woman, who had fought in vain to impose order upon wild nature at the ranch, had also discovered that 'the landscape lived, and lived as the world of the gods, unsullied and unconcerned'—a world, that is, where a god-like animal like St. Mawr would naturally take his place. The gods that the New England woman had found in 'those inner mountains' were, however, 'grim and invidious and relentless, huger than man, and lower than man,' seemingly replicas of the haughty and imposing and masterful St. Mawr himself. If Lou can be regarded as following a course parallel to that of the New England woman, then she also reaches this disquieting realm of the unseen and its supernal deities where she had envisioned St. Mawr as being. ⟨. . .⟩

In America, Lou is convinced of the truth of the revelations that came to her as she and her mother were bringing St. Mawr to America to escape emasculation. On board ship in the Gulf of Mexico, she is impressed with the beauty and grace of the porpoises: 'The marvellous beauty and fascination of natural wild things! The horror of man's unnatural life, his heaped-up civilisation!' Even in America, where there are stores of freshness and vitality, she must be alert to escape the tawdry; the second-hand intensities and superficialities of the Texas cowboys and ranch-owners, the tourist ambience of Santa Fe, the Mexicans of Santa Fe, the 'lurking, invidious Indians,' in short, the 'great weight of dirt-like inertia' enveloping the country.

In the quotation cited in the middle of the preceding paragraph, Lou expresses the rationale behind her escape from British society. She gives over the forms, manners, customs, conventions and expectations of this closed world for the openness of America (Mrs. Witt finds far greater cohesion in English life than in America), and she ardently attempts to reach 'the successive inner sanctities of herself' that are for her 'inviolable.' Like Whitman, as Lawrence described him, Lou is 'pioneering into the wilderness of unopened life.' She reaches a spiritual maturation in America despite the asceticism that she imposes upon herself, or perhaps because of it. She reacts with the fullness of the self to attain the firmest integration of the powers of the self; she reacts with intensity to the cosmic forces, and recovers some of the wonder that she had felt passing out of her life in England, where she had said: 'Oh, no, mother, I want the wonder back again, or I shall die.' The elemental quickened man whom she hopes sometime to meet would also 'breathe silence and unseen wonder.'

Lou at last knows what she wants in America and is apparently on her way to achieving it at the end of the novella: 'She wanted to be still: only that, to be very, very still, and recover her own soul.' Lou thus perceives the necessity of attaining for herself the emancipated inner being that Lawrence describes in 'Whitman': 'The soul wishes to keep clean and whole. The soul's deepest will is to preserve its own integrity, against the mind and the whole mass of disintegrating forces.' To regain the wonder and to recast her own soul, she needs the free spiritual climate of the American wilds; here she can submit to what she finds her contemporaries in Europe incapable of attaining, 'the hard, lonely responsibility of real freedom,' the true liberty that Americans can attain if they once discover it and try to fulfil its demands: 'IT [sic] being the deepest *whole* self of man, the self in its wholeness, not idealistic halfness.' In New Mexico, Lou can expect, she thinks, to see the meaningless appurtenances of her previous life dissolve, and to gain strength from identifying with 'the wild spirit' that has waited for her here for so long, a spirit that will not be gentle with her but will force her to become alive: 'But it's something big, bigger than men, bigger than people, bigger than religion. It's something to do with wild America.' Lawrence may well be dramatising here, through Lou, his own emotions as he penetrated into the culture of the North American Indian and found there a vibrant religious sensibility: 'For the whole life-effort of man was to get his life into direct contact with the elemental life of the cosmos.' Such is the thrust of Lou Witt's own adjustment to her strange adoptive land. ⟨. . .⟩

Lawrence has imagined a fable in which he dramatises with insight the dilemma of a sensitive modern woman in a world that seems to be increasingly without value. Through the symbolic thrust of St. Mawr and of the Western landscape, Lou reaches a new understanding of the self. In my view, her sincerity and her dedication make of her progression toward awareness an achieved and searching work of art. In its furthest reaches it is prophetic, in its denunciation of the barren contemporary scene, and, too, in its intimations of the process by which modern man may encounter renewal and salvation. Lou's expectations at the end of the novella do not include a present fulfilment with another person, a situation which she accepts with resignation. But she is a forerunner of those later characters who can fulfil their personal aspirations as well as their spiritual ones: Lady Chatterley, Mellors, the risen Christ and the Priestess of Isis. She demonstrates that a secure sense of the self is a needed preliminary for regeneration. For all these individuals, the readiness is all. Lou is herself ready for the full transfiguration that eludes her in *St. Mawr*.

—Frederick P. W. McDowell, "Pioneering into the Wilderness of Unopened Life: Lou Witt in America," in *The Spirit of D. H. Lawrence: Centenary Studies*, edited by Gāmini Salgādo and G. K. Das (Totowa, N. J.: Barnes & Noble Books, 1988): pp. 97–99, 100–1, 104.

Plot Summary of
"The Rocking-Horse Winner"

"The Rocking-Horse Winner," written in February 1926, belongs to Lawrence's late stories. It was originally written for an anthology, *Sixteen Stories of the Uncanny*, edited by Lady Cynthia Asquith. It is one of Lawrence's best-known and most praised stories. It is composed of intelligent dialogue and lacks the usual Lawrencian intrusions. Only the opening sentence has the resonance of a fairy tale:

> There was a woman who was beautiful, who started with all the advantages, yet she had no luck. She married for love, and the love turned to dust.

We will never learn about her difficulties or why her love has turned to dust. As for her husband, the reader gets no clue what he is like. The ridiculing exposition continues:

> She had bonny children, yet she felt they had been thrust upon her, and she could not love them. They looked at her coldly, as if they were finding fault with her.

Hester, the mother, has two little girls and a boy, Paul, "with uncanny cold fire" and enhanced sensitivity. The family lives in a pleasant house with a garden. Although they live in style, a feeling of anxiety is always in the house, because finances are tight. The house seems to be haunted by the unspoken phrase: *There must be more money*.

Most vital information in this story is given dramatically by the boy's dialogue with his mother and uncle. On one occasion Paul asks his mother, What is luck?—only to get the answer that if one is lucky one has money. He announces that he is a lucky person because God told him so.

Paul frequently rides his big rocking-horse with a frenzy. Asked about the horse's name by his uncle Oscar Cresswell, Paul responds that the horse has different names and this week it is called Sansovino. His uncle is surprised because that is the name of the horse who won the Ascott last week. It emerges that Paul often discusses horse racing with Bassett, the gardener, and they have a quite successful betting partnership thanks to the tips Paul provides.

Bassett has no clue where these tips come from, but it is clear to the reader that they come to Paul when, as he phrases it, he "get(s) there" with the help of his rocking horse.

Soon Paul, together with his uncle who has joined them, makes a substantial gain of £10,000. He arranges through the family lawyer for his mother to have an anonymous birthday present in the amount of £1,000 for five successive years. But, when she opens the letter from the lawyer, in Paul's presence, instead of the happiness Paul had anticipated, we are told that "her face hardened and became more expressionless. Then a cold, determined look came on her mouth. She hid the letter under the pile of others, and said not a word about it."

She runs to the lawyer to ask him if the whole amount of £5,000 could be advanced at once, and through the lawyer and Oscar, Paul agrees. But that will not soothe the whispering house. The voices increase, "like a chorus of frogs on a spring evening." Paul becomes overwrought trying to ensure the names of the horses for the Grand National and Lincoln races, while simultaneously studying his Latin and Greek with his tutor. He begins to lose money and, as Lawrence intimates things to come, becomes "wild-eyed and strange, as if something were going to explode in him." As the Derby, the biggest horse race of all, is drawing nearer, Paul gets more and more tense.

Two nights before the event, at a big party in town, Hester feels a sudden rush of anxiety about her son and experiences a strange seizure of uneasiness. As soon as she gets home, she rushes upstairs to his room and hears a faint noise:

The room is dark. Yet in the space near window, she hears and sees something plunging to and fro. She gazes in both fear and amusement. Then suddenly she switches on the light and sees her son, in his green pyjamas, madly surging on the rocking horse.

Paul's mysterious trance-like ecstasy has sexual and masturbatory overtones. (For further insight on this topic see Lawrence's provocative essay "Pornography and Obscenity.")

As the mother cries out to Paul, he screams in a strange voice, "It's Malabar," and falls to the ground unconscious. He remains unconscious for the next two days, occasionally repeating the name Malabar. When Bassett asks to see him on the third day, he tells him that Malabar came in first at fourteen to one and that Paul won £70,000. Paul revives briefly and proudly says to his mother, "Mother, did I ever tell you? I *am* lucky." He dies the same night.

The moral of the story is obvious. It ends ironically as the uncle comments to the mother, "You're eighty-odd thousand to the good, and a poor devil of a son to the bad. But, poor devil, poor devil, he's best gone out of life where he rides his rocking horse to find a winner." ✤

List of Characters in
"The Rocking-Horse Winner"

Paul, the hero of the story, is an oversensitive child who wants to make his mother happy. Since she constantly complains about her lack of money he takes on the responsibility to obtain some. He rides his rocking horse in a trance-like ecstasy in order to "get there" (i.e., to acquire the name of the potential horse winner at the races). He dies exhausted from his efforts.

Hester is the mother of Paul and two girls. She started with all the advantages, but her love turned to dust, and she always feels, especially when her children are present, that her heart goes hard. Although presented as greedy and insensible, she is suddenly illuminated by maternal anxiety at a party; she rushes home to check on her son.

Oscar Cresswell is Paul's uncle who joins Bassett and Paul in their betting. His comment at the end of the story ironically closes the tale.

Bassett is the family's gardener with whom Paul discusses racing. ❁

Critical Views on
"The Rocking-Horse Winner"

W. D. SNODGRASS ON THE STORY'S CHIEF STRUCTURAL
FEATURES

[W. D. Snodgrass is the author of *Heart's Needle*, a book of
poems that won the Pulitzer Prize for Poetry in 1960. In this
extract, taken from his essay "The Rocking-Horse: The
Symbol, the Pattern, the Way to Live," he investigates the
symbolic extensions of the rocking-horse itself.]

Not one member of this family really knows his wants. Like most
idealists, they have ignored the most important part of the
command *Know thyself*, and so cannot deal with their most
important problem, their own needs. To know one's needs is really
to know one's own limits, hence one's definition. Lawrence's notion
of living by "feeling" or "blood" (as opposed to "knowledge," "mind"
or "personality") may be most easily understood, perhaps, as living
according to what you *are*, not what you think you should be made
over into; knowing yourself, not external standards. Thus, what
Lawrence calls "feeling" could well be glossed as "knowing one's
wants." Paul's family, lacking true knowledge of themselves, have
turned their light, their intellect, outward, hoping to control the
external world. The mother, refusing to clarify what her emotions
really *are*, hopes to control herself and her world by acting "gentle
and anxious for her children." She tries to be or act what she thinks
she should be, not taking adequate notice of what she is and needs.
She acts from precepts about motherhood, not from recognition of
her own will, self-respect for her own motherhood. Thus, the
apparent contradiction between Hester's coldness, the "hard . . .
center of her heart," and, on the other hand, "all her tormented
motherhood flooding upon her" when Paul collapses near the end of
the story. Some deep source of affection has apparently lain hidden
(and so tormented) in her, all along; it was her business to find and
release it sooner. Similarly, Paul has a need for affection which he
does not, and perhaps cannot, understand or manage: Like his
mother, he is trying to cover this lack of self-knowledge with
knowledge about the external world, which he hopes will bring him
a fortune, and so affection.

Paul is, so, a symbol of civilized man, whipping himself on in a nervous endless "mechanical gallop," an "arrested prance," in chase of something which will destroy him if he ever catches it, and which he never really wanted anyway. He is the scientist, teacher, theorist, who must always know about the outside world so that he can manipulate it to what he believes is his advantage. Paradoxically, such knowledge comes to him only in isolation, in withdrawal from the physical world, so that his intellect may operate upon it unimpeded. And such control of the world as he can gain is useless because he has lost the knowledge of what he wants, what he is.

This, then, is another aspect of the general problem treated by the story. A still more specific form of withdrawal and domination is suggested by the names of the horses on which Paul bets. Those names—like the names of the characters—are a terrible temptation to ingenuity. One should certainly be wary of them. Yet two of them seem related to each other and strongly suggest another area into which the story's basic pattern extends. Paul's first winner, Singhalese, and his last, Malabar, have names which refer to British colonial regions of India. (A third name, Mirza, suggests "Mirzapur"—still another colonial region. But that is surely stretching things.) India is obviously one of the focal points of the modern disease of colonial empire; for years Malabar and Singhalese were winners for British stockholders and for the British people in general. The British, like any colonial power or large government or corporation, have gambled upon and tried to control peoples and materials which they never see and with which they never have any vital physical contacts. (Lawrence's essay "Men must Work and Women as Well" is significant here.) They have lived by the work of others, one of the chief evils of which is that their own physical energies have no outlet and are turned into dissatisfactions and pseudo-needs which must be filled with more and more luxuries. And so long as they "knew," placed their bets right, they were rich, were able to afford more and more dissatisfactions. A similar process destroyed Spain: a similar process destroyed Paul.

Though these last several areas of discussion are only tenuously present, most readers would agree, I think, that the rocking-horse reaches symbolically toward such meanings: into family economy and relations, into the occult, into the modern intellectual spirit, into the financial and imperial manipulations of the modern State.

But surely the sexual area is more basic to the story—is, indeed, the basic area in which begins the pattern of living which the rocking-horse symbolizes. It is precisely this area of the story and its interpretation which has been ignored, perhaps intentionally, by other commentators.

—W. D. Snodgrass, "A Rocking-Horse: The Symbol, the Pattern, the Way to Live," *Hudson Review* 11 (Summer 1958): pp. 194–96.

MICHAEL GOLDBERG ON "THE ROCKING-HORSE WINNER" AS DICKENSIAN FABLE

[This extract is taken from Michael Goldberg's essay "'The Rocking-Horse Winner': A Dickensian Fable?" published in 1969. Here he explores the parallels between Dickens's story *Dombey and Son* and Lawrence's "The Rocking-Horse Winner."]

These are, however, scattered details which serve to suggest only that there is a Dickensian influence to be found in Lawrence. Influence is, of course, a loose word—perhaps necessarily so, for the way in which an artist takes hold of aspects of another's work and makes them peculiarly his own is ultimately a mysterious process. It should be clear that I am not suggesting that *Dombey and Son* was the "source" of "The Rocking-Horse Winner," nor even that Lawrence was using it in any conscious or deliberate way. I do believe, however, that Lawrence's vision had been shaped in part by the Dickensian tradition and that in reading "The Rocking-Horse Winner" we have a strong sense of how much the Dickensian vision has penetrated the life and determined the actual way of seeing and structuring the experiences presented.

The elements of plot and their arrangement present parallels and likenesses with *Dombey and Son* too numerous to be accounted for by chance.

Both fictions feature a child named Paul whose parents are almost wholly given over to the activity of "getting on" in the world. Both children are reared in a sterile, loveless environment. Both die through the agency of some spiritual sickness whose nature it is the purpose of the tales to anatomise. Both children have an element of wizardry or a troll quality about them which enables them to penetrate the mysteries of the adult world. Both fictions employ the supernatural device of message-bearing voices—in Lawrence the house with echoes and in Dickens the whispering waves. The chosen mode of both fictions has strong affinities with fairy-tale and a good deal in common with allegory. Both are savage parables on the human sacrifice demanded by the money fetish. Thematically, both stories turn sharply on the contrast between genuine human relationships founded on love and those grounded on the cash nexus.

Besides this, there are in "The Rocking-Horse Winner," a number of Dickensian echoes which must suggest verbal reminiscence.

It seems to me, therefore, that despite its obvious difference in size, *Dombey and Son* provides a sustained series of analogues for "The Rocking-Horse Winner" and it is perhaps best for this reason to set them out in a rather systematic way.

To turn first of all to their settings, both fictions depict a middle-class environment which proves wholly unable to sustain life. Paul Dombey's birthplace "was a house of dismal state, with a circular back to it, containing a whole suite of drawing rooms looking upon a gravelled yard, where two gaunt trees, with blackened trunks and branches, rattled rather than rustled, their leaves were so smoke-dried." From this unprepossessing location Paul is removed to Mrs. Pipchin's establishment at Brighton where "the soil was more than usually chalky, flinty, and sterile."

This descriptive symbolism with its air of grotesque enchantment clearly works in the service of social criticism. The inability of the soil to yield is more truly a property of the human than the natural environment. As such it is an index to the personality of Mr. Dombey and an indictment of that part of the Victorian world he inhabits as a comfortable Philistine.

In Lawrence too, an atmosphere of brittle gentility hangs over both the physical environment and its inhabitants. The actual aridity of this world is concealed from outside inspection by a deceptive keeping up of appearances. Mr. Dombey's household glitters with a cold splendour and is a social mecca whose true character is known only to its members. Similarly, Hester and her husband "lived in style" and felt themselves despite a chronic shortage of money to be "superior to anyone in the neighborhood." The deception goes even further since to the world Hester appears the ideal mother. Only she and her children know the dreadful secret of her inadequacy.

In both fictions the setting skilfully lays the ground for the enunciation of the major theme. At the center of both stories a child named Paul is driven to his death by the inflexible money-mindedness of his parents. What both writers are urging is the idea that love of money somehow interferes with the life process. In the stark form of the parable this is illustrated through the sacrifice of a child's life to Mammon. But the child is not the sole victim of an acquisitive society. The parents, too, suffer a dreadful kind of atrophy in which Mammonism paralyzes their humanity and perverts their instinctive life, particularly their capacity for love.

Mr. Dombey, for example, at the height of his prominence suffers from a strangulation of the emotions. He can exhibit only an awkward rectitude towards his dying wife, cold hauteur towards her successor, and a withering disdain towards his daughter. For his son he feels at least a warmth related to his commercial ambition. He has to be chastened and renewed by tragic experience before feeling can flow through him again. Until that has taken place, like Lawrence's Hester, he cannot love anyone.

In such a situation it is not easy to distinguish oppressors from victims. "The Rocking-Horse Winner" is about a mother's betrayal of her son for money, status, and position. It is also about the self-betrayal of her humanity. There are perhaps resemblances between Hester and Dickens' Cleopatra to whom Lawrence refers in "Surgery for the Novel or a Bomb." Cleopatra is an ageing coquette who treats even death as though he were a beau, and her daughter as though she were a chattel virtually selling her on the marriage market to Mr. Dombey. That she is in consequence involved in a cruel dehumanising of spirit is brilliantly registered in the scene where she is laid to bed after suffering a stroke. As the false plumes of her womanhood are stripped away she is reduced to a batty and terrifying doll entirely a creature of artifice—her false eyebrows a mere extension of her pretensions to "spirit." Hester undergoes a comparable denaturing in which the elements of sexual perversity and financial desire are also mingled. Both women are inextricably entangled in the ugly paradigms of the money ethic.

—Michael Goldberg, "Lawrence's 'The Rocking-Horse Winner': A Dickensian Fable?" *Modern Fiction Studies* 15, no. 4 (Winter 1969–70): pp. 526–528, 530–531.

L. T. FITZ ON "THE ROCKING-HORSE WINNER" AND *THE GOLDEN BOUGH*

[In this extract L. T. Fitz states that the names of three horses mentioned in the story can all be found in *The Golden Bough*, the classic work on world mythology.]

Lawrence exercised some ingenuity on the names of the horses in "The Rocking-Horse Winner." Indeed, the names he chose for this strange story invite ingenuity: a name like Daffodil is interesting in the context of other sexually-charged flower imagery in Lawrence's work; a name like Lancelot is particularly tantalizing in its suggestion of ritualized, artificial love (and in view of the destructiveness of artificial love in this story, it is perhaps significant that Lancelot is a horse who loses). But most tempting is the fact that three of the seven horses named in the story bear the names of primitive tribes or the places inhabited by primitive tribes: Singhalese, Malabar, and Mirza (if we accept Mirza as a shortened form of Mirzapur). W. D. Snodgrass briefly entertains the possibility that the betting on these horses that occurs in the story has something to do with the lucrative mercantile ventures in these colonial areas during the heyday of the empire. But although the influence of *The Golden Bough* on Lawrence has been thoroughly discussed, I have not seen it mentioned that the names of these three horses (again conceding Mirza as Mirzapur) can all be found in *The Golden Bough*.

This is scarcely surprising: *The Golden Bough* is a definitive work on magic, and "The Rocking-Horse Winner" is a story about magic. The riding of a rocking horse to gain secret knowledge about real horses is an example of what Frazer calls "homeopathic magic." To say that Lawrence gained his knowledge of magic primarily from *The Golden Bough* is hardly to say anything new. Neither is there any specific relevance to the story of what Frazer says about Mirzapur or the Singhalese; they probably simply represented to Lawrence cultures with a primitive magical power appropriate to the magical events in the story. There is something very interesting, however, about what Frazer says about the people of Malabar, and since "Malabar" is the name of the last horse and Paul's dying word (it is reiterated thirteen times in the story), Lawrence's choice of this name may be significant.

One mention of Malabar in *The Golden Bough* concerns the transfer of the people's sins to a scapegoat. It is possible to see Paul in "The Rocking-Horse Winner" as the scapegoat who takes on himself the sins of his loveless family.

An even more important passage in *The Golden Bough* refers to the king of Calicut, in Malabar, who exercised godlike power for a period of twelve years, at the end of which time the king (at least in former times) was expected to cut his own throat. It is quite possible to see the relevance of this custom to the story of Paul, who is allowed to exercise his magical powers for a time but must finally (in the Faustian tradition) pay for his powers with his life.

If Lawrence was attracted, as Newman and Vickery suggest, to Frazer's portrait of the primitive dying and reviving god, perhaps he was also attracted to the tragic converse of the dying and reviving god, another Frazerian figure epitomized by the king of Malabar, the earthly potentate who receives royal power at the expense of his life. Perhaps Paul, in "The Rocking-Horse Winner," never realizes that human sacrifice is the price for his unearthly powers. The young man sacrificed at his mother's altar is not unique in the annals of Lawrence's fiction. In the works of Lawrence as in the epic work of Sir James Frazer, there are (in Newman's fine phrase) "gods who must die in the service of goddesses everywhere."

—L. T. Fitz, "'The Rocking-Horse Winner' and *The Golden Bough*," *Studies in Short Fiction* 11, no. 2 (Spring 1974): pp. 199–200.

CHARLES KOBAN ON THE MYSTICAL SIDE OF THE STORY

[In this extract Charles Koban gives credit to W. D. Snodgrass's explication of the story's meaning, but he stresses the mystical net between the mother and the son that has been overlooked by the critics.]

Hester in "The Rocking-Horse Winner" is a woman "who started with all the advantages, yet she had no luck. She married for love, and the love turned to dust." Lawrence does not describe the process of disillusionment that has occurred in Hester's marriage, but one can imagine it with the help of other of Lawrence's writings—the slow destruction of love between husband and wife in the More family, caused mainly by impecuniousness and the mother's middle-class ambitions; the disaffection that reduces love to mere passion then hatred in "England, My England," again caused by the husband's failure to be an adequate bread-winner and supporter of the family. The father in "The Rocking-Horse Winner" is clearly a failure as provider and family-head, so much so that we are scarcely conscious of his existence. He fades into the background. And his failure is aggravated by the high social position the family tries to maintain. "There was never enough money," we are told. "The mother had a small income, and the father had a small income, but not nearly enough for the social position which they had to keep up."

So when "The Rocking-Horse Winner" opens, the process of disaffection has already occurred, and the close love between husband and wife which would have generated the mystical energy necessary for the family's well-being has been transformed into an ugly passion, greed. In *Sons and Lovers*, Mrs. Morel finds an alternative to her husband's love in her closeness to her sons; and Winifred in "England, My England" finds in cold duty to her children the purpose in life which her husband fails to provide her. But Hester romanticizes the family greed into mystical love of money, as personified in the whispering house, which "came to be haunted by the unspoken phrase: *There must be more money! There must be more money!*" And her mystical abstraction communicates itself insidiously to the children, making them insecure and self-conscious just as the love between her and her husband if it still existed would have made them feel wanted and safe.

Still, Hester like Mrs. Morel and Winifred *is* closer to her children, especially Paul, than to her husband. Though she is incapable of love, she is out of a sense of duty at least solicitous for her children, for they are her link with life and vitality—with the mystical force of love that is nearly dead in her heart. What I would like to suggest is that the story can be read as the climax in the chronicle of the death of love in Hester, the death of her heart, and that as such it ought to be read primarily as an allegory of the death of the child in her, the death of innocence and love. Mystically and allegorically speaking, Paul's death is her death. At the beginning of the story we are told that "at the centre of her heart was a hard little place that could not feel love, no, not for anyone." The motif of Hester's hardness is repeated in the story though she clings to her anxiety over Paul, but by the end of the story when Paul has lapsed into a coma she is "heart-frozen." Just as Paul's eyes are like "blue stones," so his mother's heart is stonelike. "His mother sat feeling her heart had gone, turned actually into a stone." With Paul's death the death of spirit in Hester is complete, for he was her last contact with the mystical springs of love that well up in all of us only if we love some other human being, as Lawrence said, with complete "nakedness of body and spirit." The mystifying of greed is finally an empty mysticism which destroys the worshipper of money as it destroys Paul and as it destroys Hester.

The closeness between mother and son is carefully developed in the story. Their conversation and interaction make for the central human interest in the story, but the relationship is unfortunately blighted from the beginning by Hester's hardness of heart. She cares only for money and her terrible romanticism infects Paul in his solicitation for her. He is trapped in the web of mystified greed that she has woven and which she calls luck: ". . . he went about with a sort of stealth, seeking inwardly for luck. He wanted luck, he wanted it, he wanted it." Luck is money in the abstract, the mystical sense because luck will always bring money and, being divinely given, cannot (unlike money) be taken away. "'It's what causes you to have money. If you're lucky you have money. That's why it's better to be born lucky than rich.'"

The spurious mystical net is cast by the mother and the son is caught in its cords. From this point on they are one in their self-destructive mystical union. At the point when the boy is in the depths of his agony over the upcoming Derby, the union grows particularly strong and weighty—the mother's "heart curiously heavy because of him." In an interview he advises her not to be anxious about him: "I wouldn't worry, mother, if I were you." "'If you were me and I were you,' said his mother, 'I wonder what we *should* do.'" And it is so, as her response indicates: they are for the time one. The motif running throughout the story of the flaming, glaring, sometimes wild blue eyes of the boy reinforces the idea of their union. It is as if an alien spirit inhabited and drove him to seek for luck and the spirit is of course the spirit of his mother, the spirit of greed. She is inside of him, flashing out from behind "his big blue eyes blazing with a sort of madness." His madness is hers, and with his death she is left to a living death. ⟨. . .⟩

But Lawrence does not want us I think to see Paul as a kind of child-sacrifice; he scarcely wants us to see him in a moral light at all for the moral light is cast full upon Hester and by reflection upon the nearly invisible father and from them out upon our money-maddened, love-starved society. The story has to it an altogether unbelievable air, not that it lacks therefore conviction and meaning. The whispering house, the riding of a rocking-horse to find race winners, the motif of Paul's blazing, uncanny blue eyes—all give the story an eerie unreality that lifts it out of the moral realm into the sphere of mystical relationships where inexplicable forces shape our lives. Even Paul's death is finally mysterious and can only be explained as resulting from the destructive power of mystified greed in which his mother has enveloped him. Inasmuch as the boy's death marks the death of the last vestige of something vibrant, loving, and irrational in her life, it is also the death in Hester of mystical forces that sustain life while rendering it trying.

—Charles Koban, "Allegory and the Death of the Heart in 'The Rocking-Horse Winner,'" *Studies in Short Fiction* 15, no. 4 (Fall 1978): pp. 392–94, 395.

[Weldon Thornton is a professor at the University of North Carolina at Chapel Hill. He is the author of *J. M. Synge and the Western Mind* (1979), and *Antimodernism of Joyce's* Portrait of the Artist as a Young Man (1994). This extract is taken from his book *D. H. Lawrence: A Study of the Short Fiction*. Here he explains how Lawrence's story confronts us with "natural" and "supernatural" spheres, calling into question our sense of what is real.]

One persistent testimony of all his works is that when dealing with the psyche, especially with its unplumbed depths, it is not easy to draw a line between what is "realistic" and what is not. I point this out not to ameliorate the supernatural element in "The Rocking-Horse Winner," but rather to suggest that, especially given the smooth blending it achieves, the effect of "The Rocking-Horse Winner" is not to make us wonder about ghosts, but to reflect on how strange the workings of the psyche can be. ⟨...⟩

While the most overtly supernatural aspect of the story is Paul's knowledge of the winners, this is surrounded by other questionable things, of which luck and love are only two. We are told that the house is "haunted by the unspoken phrase: *There must be more money! There must be more money,*" and that the "children could hear it all the time, though nobody said it aloud." Are we to regard this voice as a "supernatural" presence? The description suggests that we do, and yet we need not invoke such an explanation. Surely we can believe that in any household the children are subtly responsive to the unspoken needs and tensions of their elders, and in this household the children readily sense their parents' need for more money.

Another questionably realistic event in this story is the mother's feeling about Paul as the crisis approaches—her "strange seizures of uneasiness about him," the "sudden anxiety about him that was almost anguish." This feeling reaches its height two nights before the Derby: she is at a party in town, when, we are told "one of her rushes of anxiety about her boy, her first-born, gripped her heart till she could hardly speak. She fought with the feeling might and main, *for she believed in common sense*. But it was too strong. She had to leave the dance and go downstairs to telephone to the country." The surprised governess assures her that all is well, but in fact it is not, for the process that will result in Paul's death has already begun. In spite of the disavowals of the opening paragraph, the mother is struggling here with her *love* of her son—something "natural" enough, but rendered problematic for her by her deep confusion of values, by her lack of faith in her capacity to love, and by her idea that these feelings violate "common sense."

In this story that plays so subtly with questions of the natural and the supernatural, the most subtle intersection between the two categories takes place in the psyche of young Paul, specifically in regard to his understanding of those crucial terms "love" and "luck." Young Paul is deeply concerned about his mother and wishes to do whatever he can to help her achieve happiness. When he comes to understand from her that the problem in their family is a lack of *luck*, his *love* for her—perhaps a "supernatural" quality, especially given the degree to which Paul feels it—takes on such intensity that it leaps the categories and becomes inordinate *luck*. With this luck, born of his desperate love, he will set right what has gone wrong in his family, the "haunting" all the children have sensed. The result is of course predictable, even before the story spells it out. Paul's inordinate luck, deriving its strength from his desperate love, is not sufficient to still the voices or set the situation in the house right. The parents' confusion of values is so deep and fundamental that it engulfs all the young boy's efforts.

All that Paul can do in response is to try harder, to transform yet more of that profound love he feels for his mother into luck. However, even his amazing store of love—the natural endowment of the child—is not sufficient to sustain an unfailing stream of luck. By trying even harder, he can still sometimes force the luck into being—though by now the demands of that process are sapping his physical as well as his psychic substance.

Young Paul tells his mother he is lucky, and subsequent events certainly bear this out: anyone who is able to beat the odds at the races and consistently pick winners is indubitably lucky. What he really means by this, however, is that he *loves* his mother so much that he is sure he can put right whatever is wrong in their family, can provide whatever she needs. His final words to his mother—

"Mother, did I ever tell you? I am lucky!"—are really a desperate, confused proclamation of his love.

This merging of the categories of real and supernatural I have been tracing is wonderfully appropriate to the underlying themes of the story. The story is about a family whose parents are so confused about their own values, about the relative importance of love and money—that is, about what is *real*—that they destroy their family. The mother is pathetically superficial, but even she has a capacity for love. Unfortunately, she does not have the insight or the faith to value and cultivate love. The father too is so confused about what is important that he cannot find his own values, much less help his wife or children find their way through the dark wood of contemporary valuelessness.

In this situation the responsibility for setting the family right, for providing what it thinks it needs, falls to the son, a boy so young he should be occupied with nothing more serious or momentous than riding his rocking horse. He is called upon to tap into his natural store of love to try to put right the terrible unhappiness and confusion of values that he and his siblings sense in their family. Given the terrible "unnatural" burden this places on him, his uncle is doubtless right when he says, "poor devil, poor devil, he's best gone out of a life where he rides his rocking-horse to find a winner."

If reading this story produces occasional shivers on the back of our neck, it is not because of its ghostly quality, but rather because of the strange intersection of "natural" and "supernatural" with which it confronts us, disturbing us by calling into question the validity, the sufficiency, of our own self-knowledge, or our knowledge of the human psyche, our sense of what is real.

—Weldon Thornton, "The Rocking-Horse Winner," in *D. H. Lawrence: A Study of the Short Fiction* (New York: Twayne Publishers, 1993): pp. 73, 75–77.

Works by
D. H. Lawrence

The White Peacock (novel). 1911

The Trespasser (novel). 1912.

Sons and Lovers (novel). 1913.

Love Poems and Others. 1913.

The Prussian Officer and Other Stories. 1914.

The Widowing of Mrs Holroyd (play). 1914.

The Rainbow (novel). 1915.

Amores. 1916.

Twilight in Italy (travel book). 1916.

Look! We Have Come Through! 1917.

New Poems. 1918.

Bay: A Book of Poems. 1919.

Women in Love (novel). 1920.

Touch and Go (play). 1920.

The Lost Girl (novel). 1920.

Tortoises (novel). 1921.

Sea and Sardinia (travel book). 1921.

Movements in European History (essays). 1921.

Psychoanalysis and the Unconscious (essays). 1921.

Fantasia of the Unconscious (essays). 1922.

Aaron's Rod (1922)

England, My England and Other Stories. 1922.

The Ladybird, The Fox, The Captain's Doll. 1923.

Studies in Classic American Literature (essays*).* 1923.

Birds, Beasts and Flowers. 1923.

Kangaroo. 1923.

The Boy in the Bush. 1924.

St. Mawr. 1925.

Reflections on the Death of a Porcupine and Other Essays (essays). 1925.

Sun. 1926.

Glad Ghosts. 1926

David (play). 1926.

The Plumed Serpent (novel). 1926.

Mornings in Mexico (travel book). 1927.

Lady Chatterley's Lover (novel). 1928.

The Collected Poems of D. H. Lawrence. 1928.

The Woman Who Rode Away and Other Stories. 1928.

The Man Who Died. 1928–29.

Rawdon's Roof. 1929.

Pornography and Obscenity (essays). 1929.

Pansies. 1929.

Nettles. 1930.

The Virgin and the Gipsy. 1930.

Love among the Haystacks and Other Pieces. 1930.

Assorted Articles (essays). 1930.

Apocalypse (essays). 1931.

Last Poems. 1932.

Etruscan Places (travel book). 1932

The Fight for Barbara (play). 1933.

A Collier's Friday Night (play). 1934.

The Married Man (play). 1940.

The Merry-go-round (play). 1941.

Works about
D. H. Lawrence

Allen, Walter. *The Short Story in English.* Oxford: Clarendon Press, 1981.

Amon, Frank. "D. H. Lawrence and the Short Story." In *The Achievement of D. H. Lawrence,* edited by Frederick J. Hoffman and Harry T. Moore. Norman: University of Oklahoma Press, 1953.

Andrews, W. T. , ed. *Critics on D. H. Lawrence.* Coral Gables, Florida: University of Miami Press, 1971.

Bates, H. E. "Lawrence and the Writers of Today." *The Modern Short Story: A Critical Survey.* London: Michael Joseph, 1972.

Bayley, John. *The Short Story: Henry James to Elizabeth Bowen.* Brighton, England: Harvester Press: 1988.

Beal, Anthony. *D. H. Lawrence.* New York: Grove Press, 1961.

Black, Michael. *D. H. Lawrence: The Early Fiction. A Commentary.* Cambridge: Cambridge University Press, 1986.

Burgess, Anthony. *Flame into Being: the Life and Work of D. H. Lawrence.* New York: Arbor Press, 1985.

Cushman, Keith. *D. H. Lawrence at Work: The Emergence of the "Prussian Officer" Stories.* Charlottesville: University Press of Virginia, 1978.

———. "The Young Lawrence and the Short Story." *Modern British Literature* 3, no. 2 (Fall 1978): 101–12.

Cushman, Keith and Jackson, Dennis, ed. *D. H. Lawrence's Literary Inheritors.* New York: Macmillan, 1991.

D. H. Lawrence Review 16, no. 3 (Fall 1983). Special Issue: D. H. Lawrence's Short Fiction.

Draper, Ronald, ed. *D. H. Lawrence: The Critical Heritage.* London: Routledge and K. Paul, 1970.

Ford, George H. *Double Measure; A Study of the Novels and Stories of D. H. Lawrence.* New York: Holt, Rinehart and Winston, 1965.

Harris, Janice Hubbard. *The Short Fiction of D . H. Lawrence.* New Brunswick, N. J.: Rutgers University Press, 1984.

Haywood, Christopher, ed. *D. H. Lawrence: New Studies.* New York: St. Martin's Press, 1987.

Hirsch, Gordon D. "The Laurentian Double: Images of D. H. Lawrence in the Stories." *D. H. Lawrence Review* 10, no. 3 (Fall 1977): 270–76.

Gamache, Lawrence, ed. *D. H. Lawrence: the Cosmic Adventure: Studies in His Ideas, Works and Literary Relationships.* Nepean, Ont.: Borealis Press, 1996.

Jackson, Dennis and Fleda Brown. *Critical Essays on D. H. Lawrence.* Boston: G. K. Hall, 1988.

Kermode, Frank. *Lawrence.* Bungay, Suffolk: Fontana/Collins, 1973.

F. R. Leavis. *Thought, Words, and Creativity: Art and Thought in Lawrence.* New York: Oxford University Press, 1976.

———. *D. H. Lawrence: Novelist.* New York: Simon and Schuster, 1955.

Moore, Harry T. *D. H. Lawrence: His Life and Works.* 2nd ed. New York: Twayne, 1964.

———. *The Priest of Love: A Life of D. H. Lawrence.* New York: Farrar, Straus, and Giroux, 1974.

Moynahan, Joseph. *The Deed of Life: The Novels and Tales of D. H. Lawrence.* Princeton, N.J.: Princeton University Press, 1963.

Niven, Alastair. *D. H. Lawrence, the Writer and His Work.* Harlow, England: British Council by Longman Group, 1980.

O'Connor, Frank. *The Lonely Voice: A Study of the Short Story.* Cleveland, Ohio: World Publishing, 1962.

Partlow, Robert and T. Harry Moore, ed. *D. H. Lawrence: The Man Who Lived. Papers Delivered at the D. H. Lawrence Conference at Southern Illinois University, Carbondale, April 1979.* Carbondale: Southern Illinois University Press, 1980.

Pinion, F. B. *D. H. Lawrence Companion: Life, Thought, and Works.* London: Macmillan, 1978.

Poirier, Richard. *A World Elsewhere: The Place of Style in American Literature.* New York: Oxford University Press, 1966.

Preston, Peter. *D. H. Lawrence, the Centre and the Circles: Essays.* Nottingham, England: 1992.

Pritchard, R. E. *D. H. Lawrence: Body of Darkness.* London: Hutchinson University Library, 1971.

Sagar, Keith, ed. *D. H. Lawrence Handbook.* Totowa, N.J.: Barnes & Noble, 1972.

———. *The Art of D. H. Lawrence.* Cambridge: Cambridge University Press, 1966.

———. *D. H. Lawrence: A Calendar of His Works.* Austin: The University of Texas Press, 1979.

———. *D. H. Lawrence: Life into Art.* Athens: University of Georgia Press, 1985.

Salgado, Gamini, and G. K. Das, eds. *The Spirit of D. H. Lawrence: Centenary Studies.* Totowa, N.J.: Barnes & Noble Books, 1988.

Scherr, Barry, J. *D. H. Lawrence Response to Plato: A Bloomian Interpretation.* New York: P. Lang, 1996.

Slade, Tony. *D. H. Lawrence.* New York: Arco Publishing, 1970.

Temple, J. "The Definition of Innocence: A Consideration of the Short Stories of D. H. Lawrence." *Studia Germanica Gandensia* 20 (1979): 105–18.

Thornton, Weldon. *D. H. Lawrence: A Study of Short Fiction.* New York: Twayne Publishers, 1993.

Wicker, Brian. *The Story-Shaped World.* London: The Athlone Press of the University of London, 1975.

Widmer, Kingsley. *The Art of Perversity.* Seattle, University of Washington Press, 1962.

Zytaruk, George. J. *D. H. Lawrence's Response to Russian Literature.* The Hague: Mouton, 1971.

Index of
Themes and Ideas